GW01607197

In diesem Buch wird die internationale Schreibweise für Akkorde benutzt. Das heißt, H wird als B und B als Bb notiert.

Satz und Layout: Tilo Müller
Fotos: LFI

BOE 7319
ISBN 3-86543-190-9
ISMN M-2016-5202-3

Printed in the EU.

www.bosworth.de

Inhalt

A Day In The Life

Words & Music by John Lennon & Paul McCartney

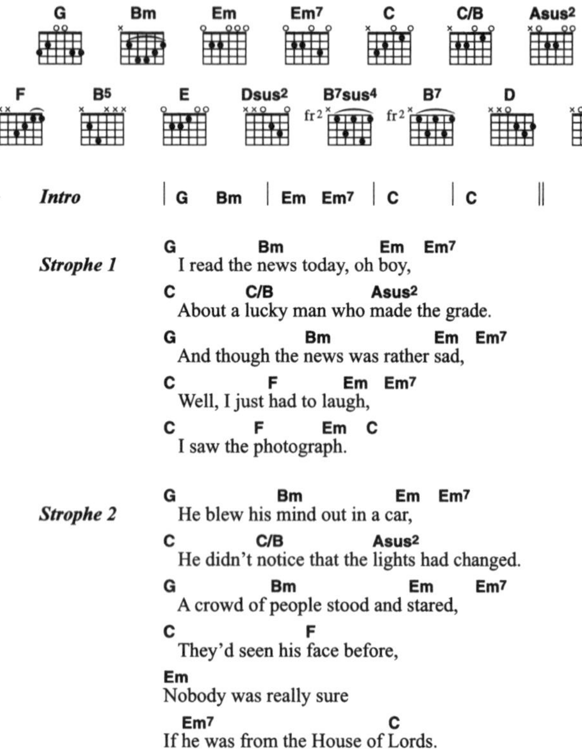

Strophe 3

```
G          Bm                 Em  Em7
  I saw a film today, oh boy,
C              C/B            Asus2
  The English army had just won the war.
G                Bm              Em    Em7
  A crowd of people turned away,
C            F           Em
  But I just had to look,
         Em7       C
Having read the book,
              N.C.(B5)
I'd love to turn you on.
```

Instrumental ||: N.C. | N.C. | N.C. | N.C. | N.C. :|| E | E ||

Bridge

```
(E)                                                     Dsus2
Woke up, got out of bed, dragged a comb across my head,
              E                       B7sus4
Found my way downstairs and drank a cup
       E              B7sus4               B7
And looking up I noticed I was late. Ha, ha, ha.
              E
Found my coat and grabbed my hat,
                              Dsus2
Made the bus in seconds flat,
              E                    B7sus4
Found my way upstairs and had a smoke
       E                                B7sus4
And somebody spoke and I went into a dream.
```

Interlude

```
C  G     D  A    E      C  G     D  A  | E D C D ||
Ah,__   ah,__   ah,__   ah,__   ah.__
```

Strophe 4

```
G            Bm                 Em  Em7
  I read the news today, oh boy,
C                  C/B                  Asus2
  Four thousand holes in Blackburn, Lancashire.
G                    Bm              Em    Em7
  And though the holes were rather small,
C             F
  They had to count them all;
Em                                  Em7                C
Now they know how many holes it takes to fill the Albert Hall.
              N.C.(B5)
I'd love to turn you on.
```

Instrumental ||: N.C. | N.C. | N.C. | N.C. | N.C. :|| E ||

A Hard Day's Night

Words & Music by John Lennon & Paul McCartney

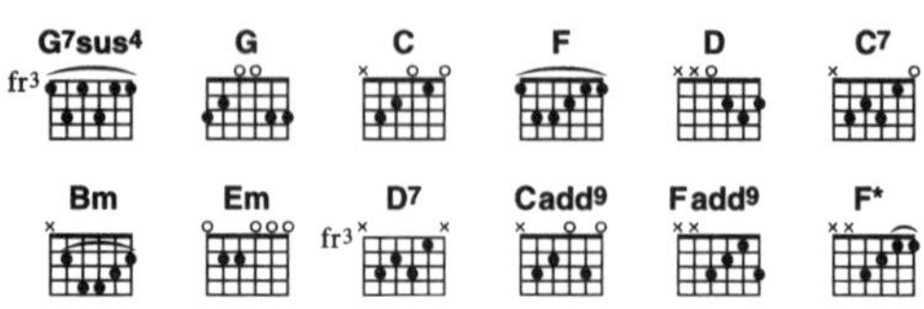

Strophe 1

G7sus4 G C G
It's been a hard day's night,
F G
And I've been working like a dog.
C G
It's been a hard day's night,
F G
I should be sleeping like a log.
C
But when I get home to you,
D
I find the things that you do,
G C7 G
Will make me feel al - right.

Strophe 2

G C G
You know I work all day,
F G
To get you money to buy you things.
C G
And it's worth it just to hear you say,
F G
You're gonna give me everything.
C
So why on earth should I moan,
D
'Cause when I get you alone,
G C7 G
You know I feel O. K.

Bridge 1

                 Bm
When I'm home
Em   Bm
Ev'rything seems to be right.
                G
When I'm home,
Em
Feeling you holding me
C7   D7
Tight, tight, yeah.

Strophe 3 As Verse 1

Instrumental |: G C | G | F | G :|

                  C
So why on earth should I moan,
                        D
'Cause when I get you alone,
                   G   C7 G
You know I feel O. K

Bridge 2

                 Bm
When I'm home
Em   Bm
Ev'rything seems to be right.
                G
When I'm home,
Em
Feeling you holding me
C7   D7
Tight, tight, yeah.

Strophe 4 Wie Strophe 1

Outro

C7   G   C7   G
  You know I feel al - right,
C7   G   Cadd9   Fadd9 F*
  You know I feel al - right.

|: Fadd9 F* | Fadd9 F* :| *Repeat to fade*

Across The Universe

Words & Music by John Lennon & Paul McCartney

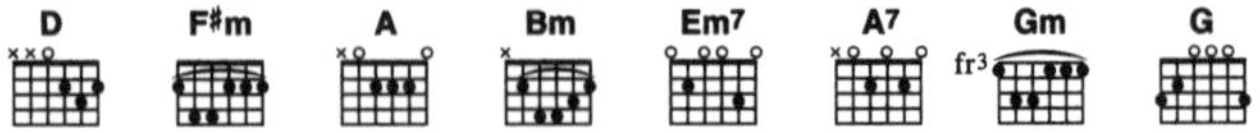

D F♯m A Bm Em7 A7 Gm G

Gitarre einen Halbton tiefer stimmen

Intro | D | F♯m | A ||

Strophe 1

D Bm F♯m
Words are flying out like endless rain into a paper cup,
Em7 A7
They slither wildly as they slip away across the universe.
D Bm F♯m
Pools of sorrow, waves of joy are drifting through my open mind,
Em7 Gm
Possessing and caressing me.

Refrain 1

D A7
Jai. Guru. Deva. Om.
A
Nothing's gonna change my world,
G D
Nothing's gonna change my world.
A
Nothing's gonna change my world,
G D
Nothing's gonna change my world.

Strophe 2

Bm F♯m Em7
Images of broken light which dance before me like a million eyes,
A7
They call me on and on across the universe.
D Bm F♯m
Thoughts meander like a restless wind inside a letter box,
Em7 A7
They tumble blindly as they make their way across the universe.

```
             D                  A7
Refrain 2    Jai. Guru. Deva. Om.
             A
             Nothing's gonna change my world,
             G                                  D
             Nothing's gonna change my world.
             A
             Nothing's gonna change my world,
             G                                  D
             Nothing's gonna change my world.

                                     Bm                  F#m
Strophe 3    Sounds of laughter, shades of life are ringing through my opened ears,
               Em7          Gm
             Inciting and inviting me.
             D            Bm                 F#m                             Em7
             Limitless, undying love which shines around me like a million suns,
                                        A7
             It calls me on and on across the universe.

             D                  A7
Refrain 3    Jai. Guru. Deva. Om.
             A
             Nothing's gonna change my world,
             G                                  D
             Nothing's gonna change my world.
             A
             Nothing's gonna change my world,
             G                                  D
             Nothing's gonna change my world.

               (D)
Outro        |: Jai. Guru. Deva. :|  Repeat to fade
```

All I've Got To Do

Words & Music by John Lennon & Paul McCartney

E11(♯5) C♯m E F♯m Am A

```
Intro         | E11(♯5)    ||

                             C♯m                 E
Strophe 1     Whenever I ____ want you around, yeah,
                           C♯m          F♯m
              All I gotta do ____ is call you on the phone

              And you'll come running home,
                  Am                   E
              Yeah, that's all I ____ gotta do.

                              C♯m              E
Strophe 2     And when I, ____ I wanna kiss you, yeah,
                           C♯m          F♯m
              All I gotta do ____ is whisper in your ear

              The words you long to hear,
                   Am            E
              And I'll ____ be kissing you.

                                         A
Refrain 1     And the same goes for me,

              Whenever you want me at all,
                   C♯m
              I'll be here, yes I will, whenever you call,
                    A                  E    C♯m
              You just gotta call on me, yeah,
                    A                  E
              You just gotta call on me.
```

Strophe 3

```
N.C.          C#m                  E
And when I, _____ I wanna kiss you, yeah,
              C#m          F#m
All I gotta do _____ is call you on the phone

And you'll come running home,
      Am                     E
Yeah,  that's all I _____  gotta do.
```

Refrain 2

```
                              A
And the same goes for me,

Whenever you want me at all,
         C#m
I'll be here, yes I will, whenever you call,
     A                      E    C#m
You just gotta call on me, yeah,
     A                      E
You just gotta call on me,
     A                      E
You just gotta call on me.
```

Outro

```
         C#m    E      C#m
Mmm. ________             Fade out
```

All My Loving

Words & Music by John Lennon & Paul McCartney

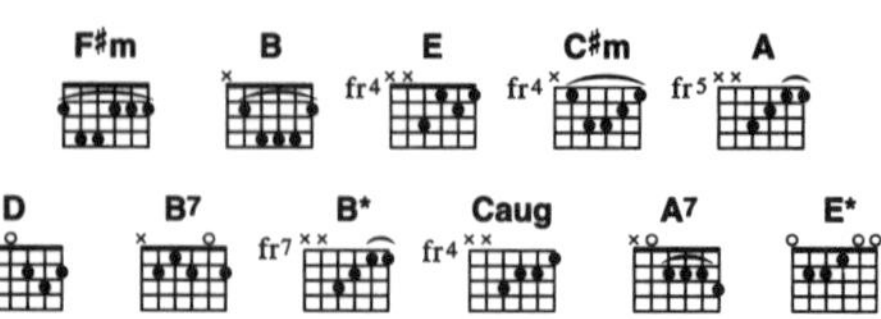

Strophe 1

N.C. F#m B
Close your eyes and I'll kiss you,
E C#m
Tomorrow I'll miss you,
A F#m D B7
Remember, I'll always be true.
F#m B
And then while I'm away
E C#m
I'll write home every day,
A B* E
And I'll send all my loving to you.

Strophe 2

N.C. F#m B
I'll pretend that I'm kissing
E C#m
The lips I am missing
A F#m D B7
And hope that my dreams will come true.
F#m B
And then while I'm away
E C#m
I'll write home every day,
A B E
And I'll send all my loving to you.

Refrain 1

C#m Caug E
All my loving I will send to you,
C#m Caug E
All my loving, darling I'll be true.

Solo | A7 | A7 | E* | E* |
| B7 | B7 | E* | E* ||

Strophe 3

```
N.C.      F#m        B
Close your eyes and I'll kiss you,
  E            C#m
Tomorrow I'll miss you,
  A             F#m      D    B7
Remember, I'll always be true.
          F#m       B
And then while I'm away
          E            C#m
I'll write home every day,
         A           B       E
And I'll send all my loving to you.
```

Refrain 2

```
       C#m   Caug         E
All my loving I will send to you,
       C#m    Caug           E
All my loving, darling I'll be true.
       C#m
All my loving,
       E
All my loving oo-ooh,
       C#m
All my loving
            E*
I will send to you.
```

All Together Now

Words & Music by John Lennon & Paul McCartney

F# G D7 C6 D6

Intro F# |: G | G | G | G :|

Strophe 1
```
G                        D7
One, two, three, four, can I have a little more?
G                                D7      G
Five, six, seven, eight, nine, ten, I love you.
```

Strophe 2
```
G            D7
A, B, C, D, can I bring my friend to tea?
G              D7      G
E, F, G, H, I, J, I love you.
```

Bridge 1
```
(Boom boom boom
C6
Boom boom boom.) Sail the ship,
G
(Boom boom boom.) Chop the tree,
C6
(Boom boom boom.) Skip the rope,
D6                D7
(Boom boom boom.) Look at me! _____

(All together now.)
```

Refrain 1
```
G
All together now, (all together now.)

All together now, (all together now.)
D7
All together now, (all together now.)
G
All together now, (all together now.)
```

Strophe 3

G D7
Black, white, green, red, can I take my friend to bed?
G D7 G
Pink, brown, yellow, orange and blue, I love you.

(All together now.)

Refrain 2

G
𝄆 All together now, (all together now.)

All together now, (all together now.)
D7
All together now, (all together now.)
G
All together now, (all together now.) 𝄇

Bridge 2

(Boom boom boom
C6
Boom boom boom.) Sail the ship,
G
(Boom boom boom.) Chop the tree,
C6
(Boom boom boom.) Skip the rope,
D6 D7
(Boom boom boom.) Look at me! _____

(All together now.)

Refrain 3

G
𝄆 All together now, (all together now.)

All together now, (all together now.)
D7
All together now, (all together now.)
G
All together now, (all together now.) 𝄇

Refrain 4

G
All together now, (all together now.)

All together now, (all together now.)
D7
All together now, (all together now.)
G
All together now. _____

All You Need Is Love

Words & Music by John Lennon & Paul McCartney

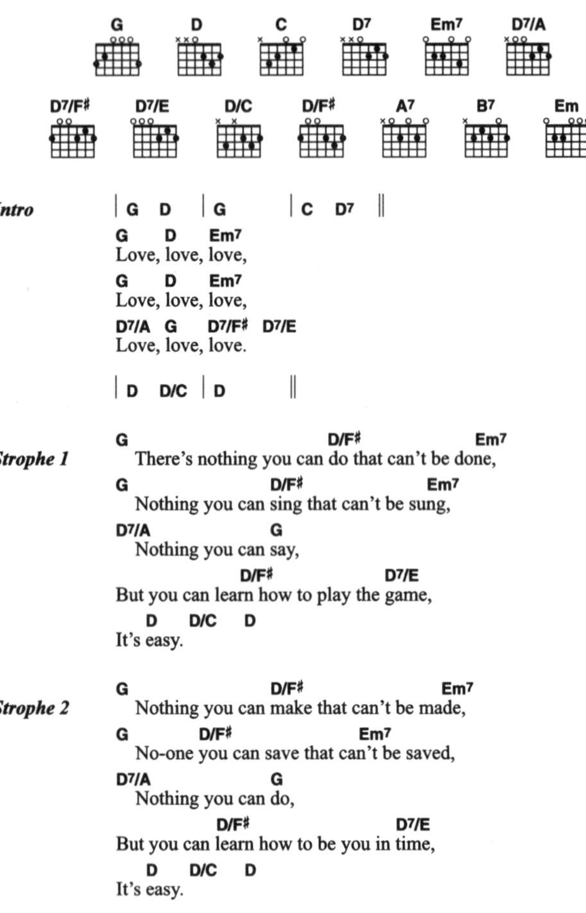

Intro | G D | G | C D7 ||

G D Em7
Love, love, love,
G D Em7
Love, love, love,
D7/A G D7/F# D7/E
Love, love, love.

| D D/C | D ||

Strophe 1

G D/F# Em7
There's nothing you can do that can't be done,
G D/F# Em7
Nothing you can sing that can't be sung,
D7/A G
Nothing you can say,
D/F# D7/E
But you can learn how to play the game,
D D/C D
It's easy.

Strophe 2

G D/F# Em7
Nothing you can make that can't be made,
G D/F# Em7
No-one you can save that can't be saved,
D7/A G
Nothing you can do,
D/F# D7/E
But you can learn how to be you in time,
D D/C D
It's easy.

Refrain 1

G A7 D D7
All you need is love,
G A7 D D7
All you need is love,
G B7 Em Em7
All you need is love, love,
C D7 G
Love is all you need.

Bridge

G D Em7
(Love, love, love,)
G D Em7
(Love, love, love,)
D7/A G D7/F# D7/E
(Love, love, love.)

| D D/C | D ||

Refrain 2

Wie Refrain 1

Strophe 3

G D/F# Em7
There's nothing you can know that isn't known,
G D/F# Em7
There's nothing you can see that isn't shown,
D7/A G
There's nowhere you can be
D/F# D7/E
That isn't where you're meant to be,
D D/C D
It's easy.

Refrain 3

Wie Refrain 1

Refrain 4

Wie Refrain 1

Coda

G
Love is all you need.

(Love is all you need.)
(G)
|: Love is all you need.

(Love is all you need.) :| *Repeat to fade*

And I Love Her

Words & Music by John Lennon & Paul McCartney

Intro | F#m | F#m | E6 | E6 ||

Strophe 1

F#m C#m
I give her all my love,
F#m C#m
That's all I do,
F#m C#m
And if you saw my love,
A B
You'd love her too,
E
I love her.

Strophe 2

F#m C#m
She gives me everything,
F#m C#m
And tenderly,
F#m C#m
The kiss my lover brings,
A B
She brings to me,
E
And I love her.

Bridge

C#m B
A love like ours
C#m G#m
Could never die
C#m G#m
As long as I
B B7
Have you near me.

Strophe 3

```
F♯m                 C♯m
   Bright are the stars that shine,
F♯m             C♯m
   Dark is the sky,
F♯m              C♯m
   I know this love of mine
A                B
   Will never die,
        E
And I love her.
```

Solo

| Gm | Dm | Gm | Dm | Gm |
| Dm | B♭ | C | F | F ||

Strophe 4

```
Gm                  Dm
   Bright are the stars that shine,
Gm              Dm
   Dark is the sky,
Gm               Dm
   I know this love of mine
B♭               C
   Will never die,
        F
And I love her.
```

Coda

| Gm | Gm | F | F |
| Gm | Gm | D ||

And Your Bird Can Sing

Words & Music by John Lennon & Paul McCartney

D Em G F♯m

F♯m(maj7) F♯m7 B7 A G/D

Kapo zweiter Bund

Intro | D | D | D | D ||

```
*Strophe 1*     D
                You tell me that you've got everything you want,

                And your bird can sing,
                                    Em
                But you don't get me,
                G                 D
                   You don't get   me.
```

```
*Strophe 2*     D
                You say you've seen seven wonders,

                And your bird is green,
                                    Em
                But you can't see me,
                G                 D
                   You can't see   me.
```

```
*Bridge 1*      F♯m                    F♯m(maj7)
                When your prized possessions
                F♯m7                B7
                Start to weigh you down,
                D               Em
                Look in my direction,
                                         A
                I'll be 'round, I'll be 'round.
```

Solo 1 | D | D | D | D |
| Em | G | D | D ||

Bridge 2
F♯m F♯m(maj7)
When your bird is broken,
F♯m7 B7
Will it bring you down?
D Em
You may be awoken,
A
I'll be 'round, I'll be 'round,

Strophe 3
D
You tell me that you've heard every sound there is,

And your bird can swing,
Em
But you can't hear me,
G D
You can't hear me.

Solo 2 | D | D | D | D |
| Em | G | D | D ||

Coda | D | D | D | G/D ||

Any Time At All

Words & Music by John Lennon & Paul McCartney

Bm D A G Dsus4

Dsus2 F#m/C# Gm/B♭ D/A A7

```
               N.C.            Bm    D
Refrain 1      Any time at all,
                               A
               Any time at all,
                               Bm
               Any time at all,
                                    G
               All you've got to do is call
                    A     Dsus4  D  Dsus2  D
               And I'll be there.

               D                     F#m/C#
Strophe 1         If you need somebody to love,
               Bm                     Gm/B♭
                  Just look into my eyes,
               D/A           A             D
               I'll be there to make you feel right.

                                  F#m/C#
Strophe 2      If you're feeling sorry and sad,
               Bm                    Gm/B♭
                  I'd really sympathise.
               D/A                      A           Dsus4  D  Dsus2  D
               Don't you be sad, just call me tonight.
```

Refrain 2 Wie Refrain 1

Strophe 3

D F♯m/C♯
If the sun has faded away,
Bm Gm/B♭
I'll try to make it shine.
D/A A D
There is nothing I won't do.

Strophe 4

F♯m/C♯
When you need a shoulder to cry on,
Bm Gm/B♭
I hope it will be mine.
D/A A Dsus4 D Dsus2 D
Call me tonight, and I'll come to you.

Refrain 3

Wie Refrain 1

Solo

| A | A7 | A | A7 | G | A |
| G | A | Dsus4 D Dsus2 | D ||

Refrain 4

N.C. Bm D
Any time at all,
A
Any time at all,
Bm
Any time at all,
G
All you've got to do is call
A Dsus4 D Dsus2 D
And I'll be there.
G
Any time at all,
A
All you've got to do is call
Dsus4 D Dsus2 D
And I'll be there.

Baby's In Black

Words & Music by John Lennon & Paul McCartney

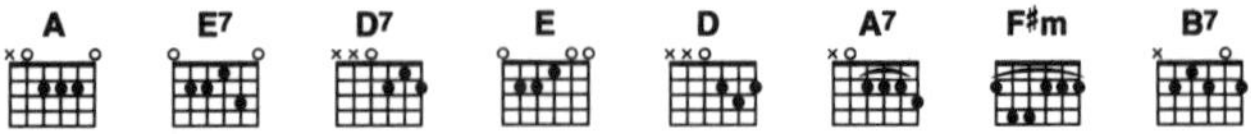

A E7 D7 E D A7 F♯m B7

Intro | (A) (A/E) | A ||

Refrain 1

```
A          E7
Oh dear, what can I do?
D7                           E
Baby's in black and I'm feeling blue,
            A   D            A
Tell me, oh, what can I do?
```

Strophe 1

```
A
She thinks of him,
      A7                   D
And so she dresses in black,
                                A
And though he'll never come back,
E               A
She's dressed in black.
```

Refrain 2 Wie Refrain 1

Strophe 2

```
A
I think of her,
      A7                  D
But she thinks only of him,
                             A
And though it's only a whim,
E              A
She thinks of him.
```

Bridge 1

```
F♯m      B7
Oh, how long will it take,
D        E7                          A
Till she sees the mistake she has made.
```

Refrain 3

```
         E7
Oh dear, what can I do?
D7                  E
Baby's in black and I'm feeling blue,
         A  D       A
Tell me, oh, what can I do?
```

Solo

| A | E | D | E | A D | A ||

Bridge 2

```
F♯m      B7
Oh, how long will it take,
D       E7                     A
Till she sees the mistake she has made.
```

Refrain 4

```
      E7
Dear, what can I do?
D7                  E
Baby's in black and I'm feeling blue,
         A  D       A
Tell me, oh, what can I do?
```

Strophe 3

```
A
She thinks of him,
    A7             D
And so she dresses in black,
                             A
And though he'll never come back,
E             A
She's dressed in black.
```

Refrain 5

```
A        E7
Oh dear, what can I do?
D7                  E
Baby's in black and I'm feeling blue,
         A  D       A
Tell me, oh, what can I do?
```

Back In The USSR

Words & Music by John Lennon & Paul McCartney

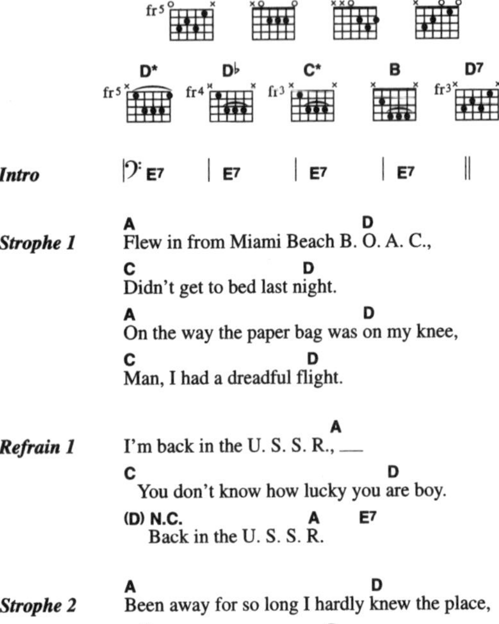

Intro | E7 | E7 | E7 | E7 ||

Strophe 1

A D
Flew in from Miami Beach B. O. A. C.,
C D
Didn't get to bed last night.
A D
On the way the paper bag was on my knee,
C D
Man, I had a dreadful flight.

Refrain 1

A
I'm back in the U. S. S. R., —
C D
You don't know how lucky you are boy.
(D) N.C. A E7
Back in the U. S. S. R.

Strophe 2

A D
Been away for so long I hardly knew the place,
C D
Gee it's good to be back home.
A D
Leave it till tomorrow to unpack my case,
C D
Honey, disconnect the phone.

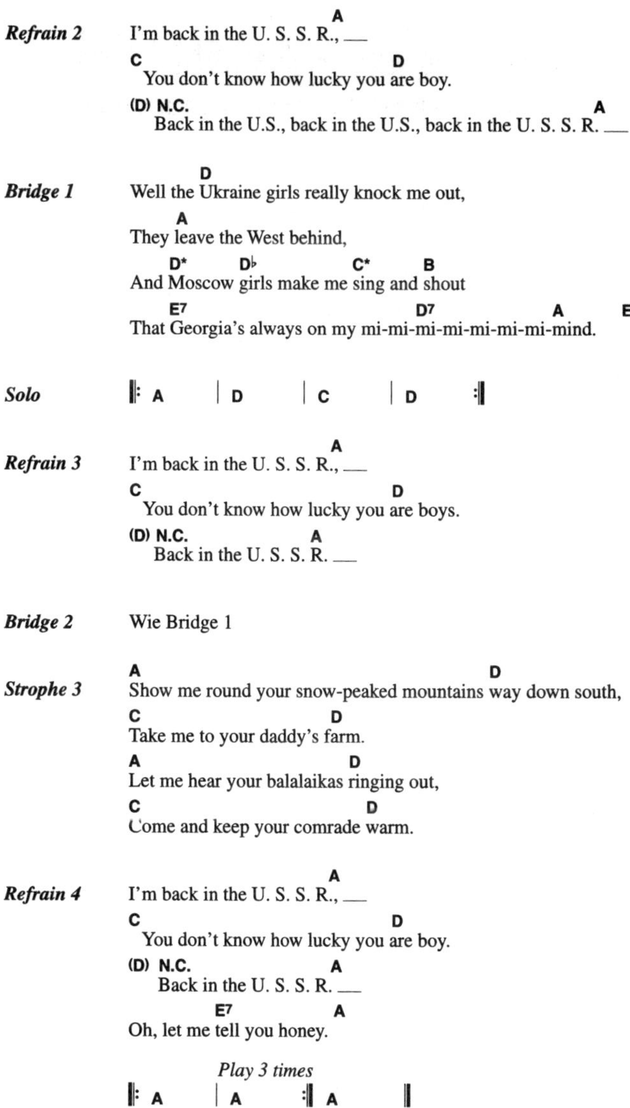

Refrain 2

A
I'm back in the U. S. S. R., __
C D
You don't know how lucky you are boy.
(D) N.C. A
Back in the U.S., back in the U.S., back in the U. S. S. R. __

Bridge 1

D
Well the Ukraine girls really knock me out,
A
They leave the West behind,
D* D♭ C* B
And Moscow girls make me sing and shout
E7 D7 A E7
That Georgia's always on my mi-mi-mi-mi-mi-mi-mi-mind.

Solo

|: A | D | C | D :|

Refrain 3

A
I'm back in the U. S. S. R., __
C D
You don't know how lucky you are boys.
(D) N.C. A
Back in the U. S. S. R. __

Bridge 2

Wie Bridge 1

Strophe 3

A D
Show me round your snow-peaked mountains way down south,
C D
Take me to your daddy's farm.
A D
Let me hear your balalaikas ringing out,
C D
Come and keep your comrade warm.

Refrain 4

A
I'm back in the U. S. S. R., __
C D
You don't know how lucky you are boy.
(D) N.C. A
Back in the U. S. S. R. __
E7 A
Oh, let me tell you honey.

Play 3 times

|: A | A :| A ||

Because

Words & Music by John Lennon & Paul McCartney

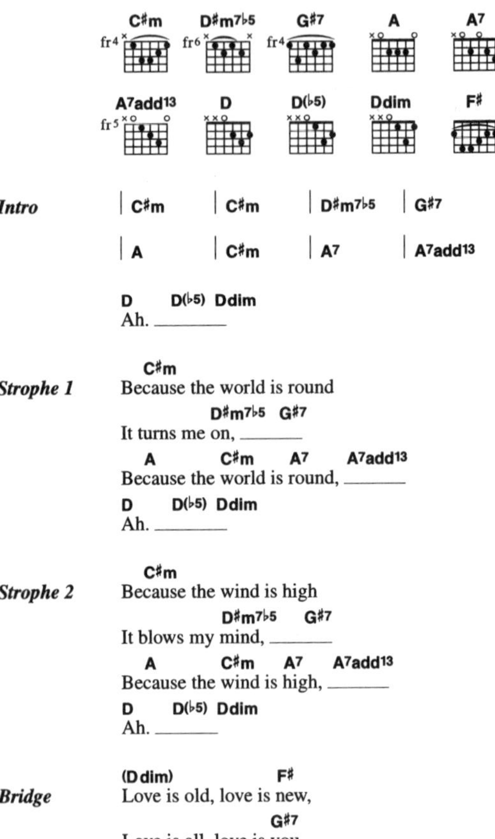

Intro

| C#m | C#m | D#m7♭5 | G#7 |
| A | C#m | A7 | A7add13 ||

D D(♭5) Ddim
Ah. ______

Strophe 1

C#m
Because the world is round
D#m7♭5 G#7
It turns me on, ______
A C#m A7 A7add13
Because the world is round, ______
D D(♭5) Ddim
Ah. ______

Strophe 2

C#m
Because the wind is high
D#m7♭5 G#7
It blows my mind, ______
A C#m A7 A7add13
Because the wind is high, ______
D D(♭5) Ddim
Ah. ______

Bridge

(Ddim) F#
Love is old, love is new,
G#7
Love is all, love is you.

Strophe 3

C#m
Because the sky is blue

D#m7♭5 G#7
It makes me cry, ______

A C#m A7 A7add13
Because the sky is blue, ______

D D(♭5) Ddim
Ah. __________

Instrumental

| C#m | C#m | D#m7♭5 | G#7 |
(Ah.) __ (Ah.) __________

| A | C#m | A7 | A7add13 |
(Ah.) __ Ah. __________

| D | D(♭5) Ddim ||
Ah. __________

Birthday

Words & Music by John Lennon & Paul McCartney

A7 D7 E7 E C G A

Intro | (A7) | (A7) | (A7) | (A7) | (D7) | (D7) |
| (A7) | (A7) | (E7) | (E7) | (A7) | (A7) ||

Strophe 1

```
A7       N.C.
  You say it's your birthday,
A7 N.C.
It's my birthday too, yeah.
D7       N.C.
  You say it's your birthday,
A7          N.C.
  We're gonna have a good time.
E7       N.C.
  I'm glad it's your birthday,
A7           N.C.
  Happy birthday to you.
```

| 8 Takte Drums | E | E ||

Bridge

```
E
  Yes, we're going to a party, party,

Yes, we're going to a party, party,

Yes, we're going to a party, party.
```

Refrain 1

```
C            G
  I would like you to dance,
C                    G
(Birthday) Take a cha-cha-cha-chance,
C                         G
(Birthday) I would like you to dance,
C              G       E
(Birthday) Dance! _____
```

Instrumental | (A7) | (A7) | (A7) | (A7) | (D7) | (D7) |

| (A7) | (A7) | (E7) | (E7) | (A7) | (A7) |

| (A) | (A) (G) | (A) | (A) (G) ||

Refrain 2

C G
I would like you to dance,
C G
(Birthday) Take a cha-cha-cha-chance,
C G
(Birthday) I would like you to dance,
C G E
(Birthday) Dance! ____

Strophe 2

A7
You say it's your birthday,

It's my birthday too, yeah.
D7
You say it's your birthday,
A7
We're gonna have a good time.
E7
I'm glad it's your birthday,
A7
Happy birthday to you.

Coda | A | A ||

Blackbird

Words & Music by John Lennon & Paul McCartney

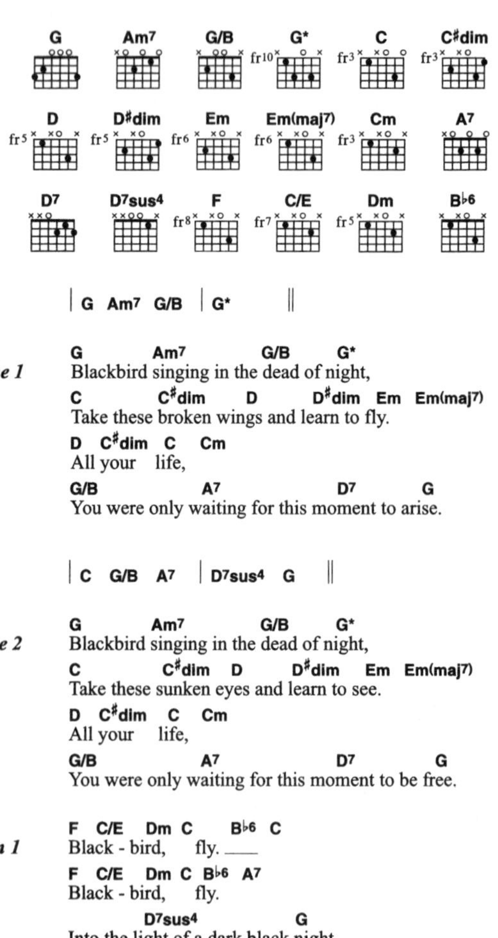

Intro | G Am7 G/B | G* ||

Strophe 1

```
G              Am7            G/B        G*
Blackbird singing in the dead of night,
C              C#dim        D            D#dim   Em   Em(maj7)
Take these broken wings and learn to fly.
D   C#dim  C    Cm
All your    life,
G/B                  A7                      D7          G
You were only waiting for this moment to arise.
```

| C G/B A7 | D7sus4 G ||

Strophe 2

```
G              Am7            G/B        G*
Blackbird singing in the dead of night,
C              C#dim    D          D#dim     Em   Em(maj7)
Take these sunken eyes and learn to see.
D   C#dim   C    Cm
All your     life,
G/B                  A7                      D7             G
You were only waiting for this moment to be free.
```

Refrain 1

```
F   C/E    Dm  C      B♭6  C
Black - bird,     fly. ___
F   C/E    Dm  C  B♭6  A7
Black - bird,     fly.
           D7sus4               G
Into the light of a dark black night.
```

Bridge 1

| G Am7 G/B | G* | C C♯dim D D♯dim | Em Em(maj7) |
(night.)
| D C♯dim | C Cm | G/B A7 | D7sus4 G ||

Refrain 2

F C/E Dm C B♭6 C
Black - bird, fly. ___
F C/E Dm C B♭6 A7
Black - bird, fly.
D7sus4 G
Into the light of a dark black night.

Bridge 2

| G Am7 G/B | G* | G | G |
(night.)

| G Am7 G/B | C G/B A7 | D7sus4 ||

Strophe 3

G Am7 G/B G*
Blackbird singing in the dead of night,
C C♯dim D D♯dim Em Em(maj7)
Take these broken wings and learn to fly.
D C♯dim C Cm
All your life,
G/B A7 D7sus4 G
You were only waiting for this moment to arise.

Coda

C G/B A7 D7sus4 G
You were only waiting for this moment to arise.
C G/B A7 D7sus4 G
You were only waiting for this moment to arise.

Can't Buy Me Love

Words & Music by John Lennon & Paul McCartney

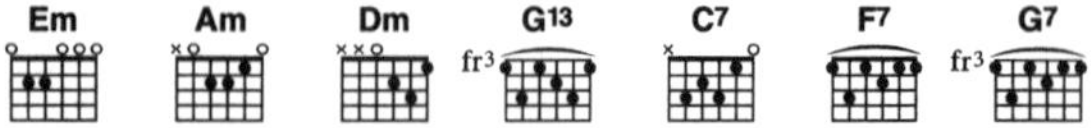

Em Am G13 Dm C7 F7 G7

Intro

Em Am Em Am
Can't buy me love, ___ love, ___

Dm G13
Can't buy me love. ___

Strophe 1

C7
I'll buy you a diamond ring my friend,

If it makes you feel alright.

F7
I'll get you anything my friend,

C7
If it makes you feel alright.

G7 F7
'Cos I don't care too much for money,

C7
(For) money can't buy me love.

Strophe 2

C7
I'll give you all I've got to give,

If you say you love me too.

F7
I may not have a lot to give,

C7
But what I've got I'll give to you.

G7 F7
I don't care too much for money.

C7
(For) money can't buy me love.

Refrain 1

Em Am
Can't buy me love, ___
C7
Everybody tells me so.
Em Am
Can't buy me love, ___
Dm G13
No, no, no, no.

Strophe 3

C7
Say you don't need no diamond rings

And I'll be satisfied.
F7
Tell me that you want the kind of things
C7
That money just can't buy.
G7 F7
I don't care too much for money.
C7
(For) money can't buy me love.

Solo

C7	C7	C7	C7
F7	F7	C7	C7
G7	F7	C7	C7	

Refrain 2

Wie Refrain 1

Strophe 4

Wie Strophe 3

Outro

Em Am Em Am
Can't buy me love, ___ love, ___
Dm G13
Can't buy me love ___
C7
Oh.

Come Together

Words & Music by John Lennon & Paul McCartney

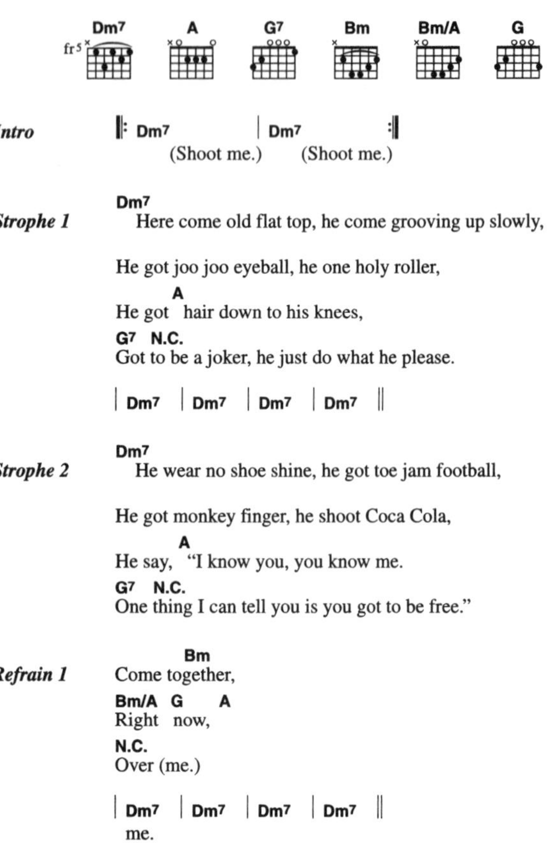

Strophe 3

```
Dm7
   He bag production, he got walrus gumboot,

He got Ono sideboard, he one spinal cracker,
         A
He got   feet down below his knee,
G7    N.C.
Hold you in his armchair, you can feel his disease.
```

Refrain 2

```
            Bm
Come together,
Bm/A  G     A
Right   now,
N.C.
Over (me.)

| Dm7      | Dm7     || Dm7     | Dm7     | Dm7     | Dm7      |
  me.              (Right!)                          (Come.)

| A        | A       | A       | A       | Dm7     | Dm7      ||
 (Come.)
```

Strophe 4

```
Dm7
   He roller coaster, he got early warning,

He got muddy water, he one mojo filter,
          A
He say,   "One and one and one is three."
G7   N.C.
Got to be good looking 'cause he's so hard to see.
```

Refrain 3

```
            Bm
Come together,
Bm/A  G     A
Right   now,
N.C.
Over (me.)

| Dm7     | Dm7     | Dm7     | Dm7     || Dm7     | Dm7     |
  me.                                Oh!
```

Coda

```
    Dm7
|:    Come together, yeah!  :|
```
Repeat to fade

Day Tripper

Words & Music by John Lennon & Paul McCartney

E7 A7 F#7 A7* G#7 C#7 B7

Intro | (E7) | (E7) |: E7 | E7 | E7 | E7 :|

```
              E7
*Strophe 1*   Got a good reason

              For taking the easy way out.
              A7
              Got a good reason
                    E7
              For taking the easy way out, now.
                               F#7
              She was a day tripper,

              One way ticket, yeah.
                                A7*  G#7          C#7
              It took me so   long to find out,
                                  B7
              And I found out.

              | (E7) | (E7) | E7 | E7 ||

              E7
*Strophe 2*   She's a big teaser,

              She took me half the way there,
              A7
              She's a big teaser,
              E7
              She took me half the way there, now.
```

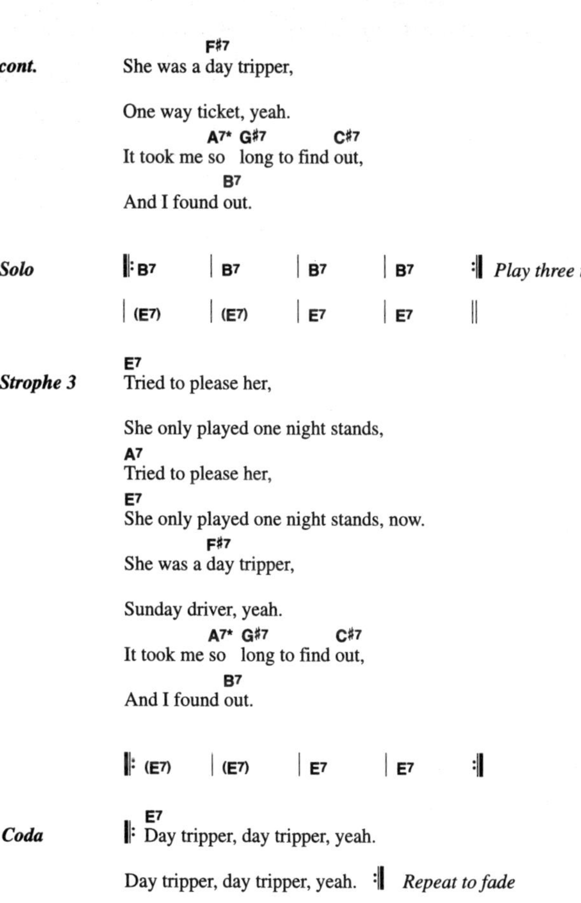

cont.

F#7
She was a day tripper,

One way ticket, yeah.

A7* G#7 C#7
It took me so long to find out,

B7
And I found out.

Solo

|: B7 | B7 | B7 | B7 :| *Play three times*

| (E7) | (E7) | E7 | E7 ||

Strophe 3

E7
Tried to please her,

She only played one night stands,

A7
Tried to please her,

E7
She only played one night stands, now.

F#7
She was a day tripper,

Sunday driver, yeah.

A7* G#7 C#7
It took me so long to find out,

B7
And I found out.

|: (E7) | (E7) | E7 | E7 :|

Coda

E7
|: Day tripper, day tripper, yeah.

Day tripper, day tripper, yeah. :| *Repeat to fade*

Doctor Robert

Words & Music by John Lennon & Paul McCartney

A7 Asus4 F#7 E7 B E/B

Intro | A7 Asus4 | A7 Asus4 | A7 Asus4 | A7 Asus4 ||

Strophe 1

```
A7
Ring my friend, I said you'd call, Doctor Robert.

Day or night, he'll be there any time at all, Doctor Robert.
           F#7
Doctor Robert, you're a new and better man,

He helps you to understand,
            E7                 F#7          B
He does everything he can, Doctor Robert.
```

Strophe 2

```
A7
If you're down, he'll pick you up, Doctor Robert.

Take a drink from his special cup, Doctor Robert.
           F#7
Doctor Robert, he's a man you must believe,

Helping anyone in need,
E7                  F#7               B
No-one can succeed like Doctor Robert.
```

Bridge 1

```
B                              E/B     B
Well, well, well, you're feeling fine,
                            E/B
Well, well, well, he'll make you,
           A7
Doctor Robert.
```

Strophe 3

```
A7
My friend works for the National Health, Doctor Robert.

You'll pay money just to see yourself with Doctor Robert.
       F#7
Doctor Robert, you're a new and better man,

He helps you to understand,
        E7           F#7     B
He does everything he can, Doc Robert.
```

Bridge 2

```
B                      E/B   B
Well, well, well, you're feeling fine,
                      E/B
Well, well, well, he'll make you,
       A7
Doctor Robert.
```

Coda

```
A7
Ring my friend, I said you'd call

Doctor Robert.

Ring my friend, I said you'd call

Doc Robert.
       F#7     B
Doctor Robert!  Fade out
```

Don't Let Me Down

Words & Music by John Lennon & Paul McCartney

Intro | E Esus4 | E ||

Refrain 1

F♯m
Don't let me down,
E Esus4 E
Don't let me down,
F♯m
Don't let me down,
E Esus4 E
Don't let me down.

Strophe 1

N.C. F♯m7
Nobody ever loved me like she does,
Emaj7 Esus4 E
Ooh she does, yes she does,
N.C. F♯m7
And if somebody loved me like she do me,
Emaj7 Esus4 E
Ooh she do me, yes she does.

Refrain 2

F♯m
Don't let me down,
E Esus4 E
Don't let me down,
F♯m
Don't let me down,
E Esus4 E
Don't let me down.

Bridge 1

N.C. E
I'm in love for the first time,
B7
Don't you know it's going to last.

It's a love that lasts forever,
E Esus4 E
It's a love that has no past.

Refrain 3

F#m
Don't let me down,
E Esus4 E
Don't let me down,
F#m
Don't let me down,
E Esus4 E
Don't let me down.

Strophe 2

N.C. F#m7
And from the first time that she really done me,
Emaj7 Esus4 E
Ooh, she done me, she done me good.
N.C. F#m7
I guess nobody ever really done me,
Emaj7 Esus4 E
Ooh she done me, she done me good.

Refrain 4

F#m
Don't let me down, hey!
E Esus4 E
Don't let me down,
F#m
Don't let me down,
E Esus4 E
Don't let me down.
F#m E Esus4 E
Don't let me down,
F#m
Don't let me down.

Can you dig it?
E Esus4 E
Don't let me down.

Drive My Car

Words & Music by John Lennon & Paul McCartney

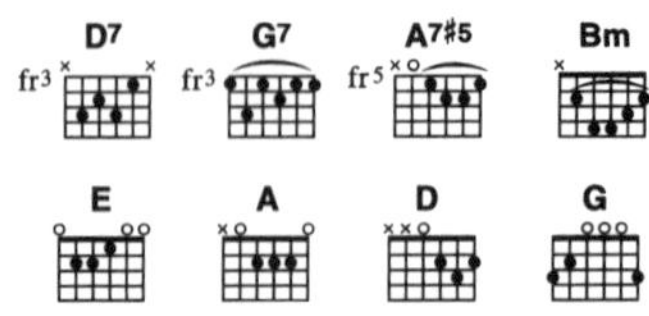

Intro | (D7) | (D7) ||

Strophe 1

```
D7                        G7
   Asked a girl what she wanted to be,
D7                   G7
   She said, „Baby, can't you see?
D7                        G7
   I wanna be famous, a star of the screen,
    A7#5
But you can do something in between."
```

Refrain 1

```
Bm                          G7  Bm                  G7
Baby, you can drive my car, yes I'm gonna be a star,
Bm                          E     A        D         G  A
Baby, you can drive my car, and maybe I'll love you.
```

Strophe 2

```
D7                        G7
   I told that girl that my prospects were good,
D7                        G7
   She said, „Baby, it's understood.
D7                          G7
   Working for peanuts is all very fine,
    A7#5
But I can show you a better time."
```

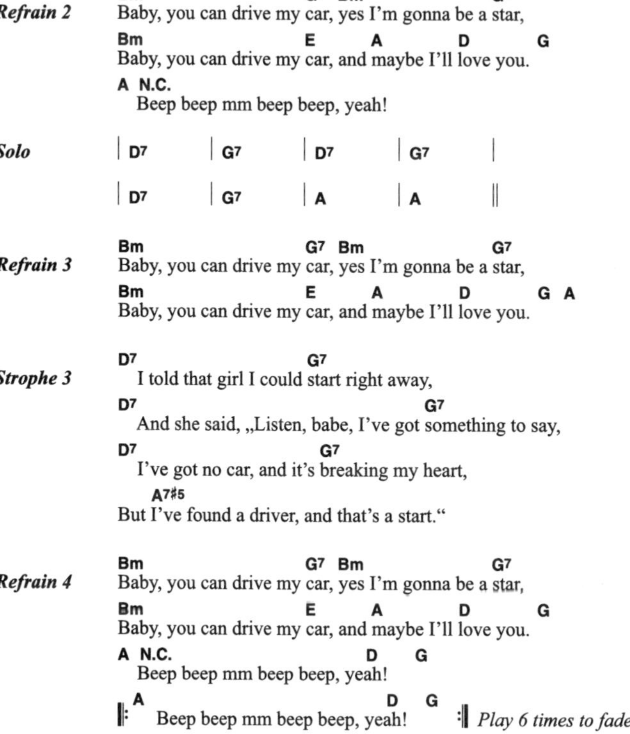
Refrain 2
Bm G7 Bm G7
Baby, you can drive my car, yes I'm gonna be a star,
Bm E A D G
Baby, you can drive my car, and maybe I'll love you.
A N.C.
Beep beep mm beep beep, yeah!
Solo
| D7 | G7 | D7 | G7 |
| D7 | G7 | A | A ||
Refrain 3
Bm G7 Bm G7
Baby, you can drive my car, yes I'm gonna be a star,
Bm E A D G A
Baby, you can drive my car, and maybe I'll love you.
Strophe 3
D7 G7
I told that girl I could start right away,
D7 G7
And she said, „Listen, babe, I've got something to say,
D7 G7
I've got no car, and it's breaking my heart,
A7♯5
But I've found a driver, and that's a start."
Refrain 4
Bm G7 Bm G7
Baby, you can drive my car, yes I'm gonna be a star,
Bm E A D G
Baby, you can drive my car, and maybe I'll love you.
A N.C. D G
Beep beep mm beep beep, yeah!
A D G
Beep beep mm beep beep, yeah!
Play 6 times to fade

Eight Days A Week

Words & Music by John Lennon & Paul McCartney

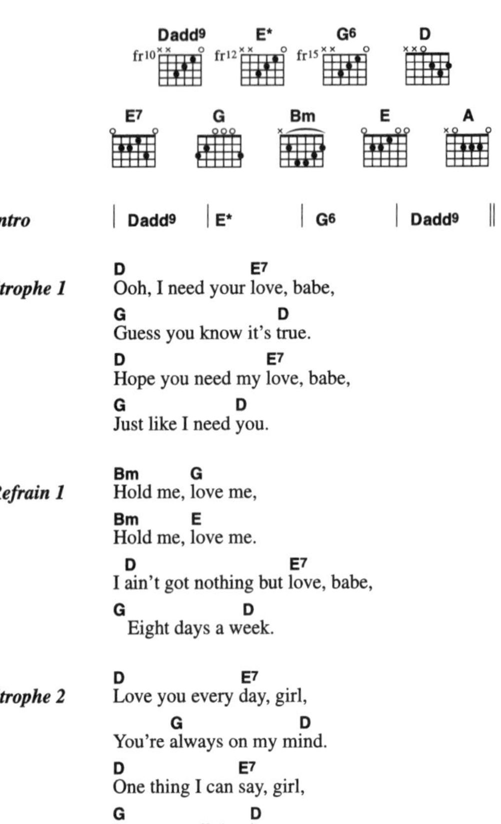

Intro | Dadd9 | E* | G6 | Dadd9 ||

Strophe 1

D E7
Ooh, I need your love, babe,
G D
Guess you know it's true.
D E7
Hope you need my love, babe,
G D
Just like I need you.

Refrain 1

Bm G
Hold me, love me,
Bm E
Hold me, love me.
D E7
I ain't got nothing but love, babe,
G D
Eight days a week.

Strophe 2

D E7
Love you every day, girl,
G D
You're always on my mind.
D E7
One thing I can say, girl,
G D
Love you all the time.

Refrain 2

Bm G
Hold me, love me,
Bm E
Hold me, love me.
D E7
I ain't got nothing but love, girl,
G D
Eight days a week.

Bridge 1

A
Eight days a week,
Bm
I love ___ you.
E
Eight days a week
G A
Is not enough to show I care.

Strophe 3 Wie Strophe 1

Refrain 3 Wie Refrain 1

Bridge 2 Wie Bridge 1

Strophe 4 Wie Strophe 2

Refrain 4

Bm G
Hold me, love me,
Bm E
Hold me, love me,
D E7
I ain't got nothing but love, girl,
G D
Eight days a week.
G D
Eight days a week.
G D
Eight days a week.

Outro | Dadd9 | E* | G6 | Dadd9 ||

Eleanor Rigby

Words & Music by John Lennon & Paul McCartney

C   Em   Em7*   Em7   Em6   Em aug

Intro

C   Em
Ah, look at all the lonely people!
C   Em
Ah, look at all the lonely people!

Strophe 1

Em
Eleanor Rigby,
                                                                        C
Picks up the rice in the church where a wedding has been,
               Em
Lives in a dream. ____

Waits at the window,
                                                   Em7*   C
Wearing a face that she keeps in a jar by the door,
             Em
Who is it for?

Refrain 1

Em7   Em6   Em aug   Em
All the lonely people, where do they all come from?
Em7   Em6   Em aug   Em
All the lonely people, where do they all belong?

Strophe 2

Em
Father McKenzie,
                                                                   C
Writing the words of a sermon that no-one will hear,
                 Em
No-one comes near.

Look at him working,
                                                                        C
Darning his socks in the night when there's nobody there,
                 Em
What does he care?

```
               Em7            Em6           Emaug             Em
*Refrain 2*    All the lonely people, where do they all come from?
               Em7            Em6           Emaug       Em
               All the lonely people, where do they all belong?

               C                          Em
*Bridge*       Ah, look at all the lonely people!
               C                          Em
               Ah, look at all the lonely people!

               Em
*Strophe 3*    Eleanor Rigby
                                                                C
               Died in the church and was buried along with her name,
                      Em
               Nobody came.

               Father McKenzie,
                                                                   C
               Wiping the dirt from his hands as he walks from the grave,
                          Em
               No-one was saved.

               Em7            Em6           Emaug             Em
*Refrain 3*    All the lonely people, where do they all come from?
               Em7            Em6           Emaug       Em
               All the lonely people, where do they all belong?
```

Every Little Thing

Words & Music by John Lennon & Paul McCartney

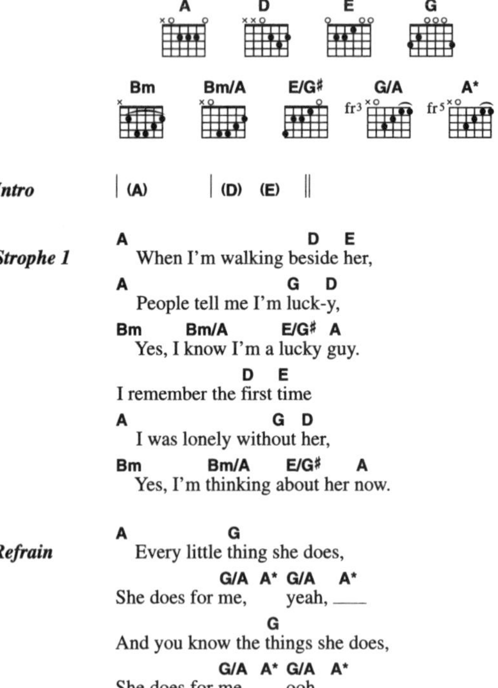

Intro | (A) | (D) (E) ||

Strophe 1

```
A                        D   E
   When I'm walking beside her,
A                     G    D
   People tell me I'm luck-y,
Bm        Bm/A       E/G♯  A
   Yes, I know I'm a lucky guy.
                   D    E
I remember the first time
A                   G    D
   I was lonely without her,
Bm           Bm/A     E/G♯     A
   Yes, I'm thinking about her now.
```

Refrain

```
A               G
   Every little thing she does,
                G/A  A*  G/A    A*
She does for me,         yeah, ____
                         G
And you know the things she does,
                G/A  A*  G/A   A*
She does for me,         ooh. ____
```

Strophe 2

```
A                              D   E
   When I'm with her I'm hap-py,
A                         G     D
   Just to know that she loves me,
Bm      Bm/A          E/G#      A
   Yes I know that she loves me now.
                          D    E
There is one thing I'm sure of,
A                   G  D
   I will love her forev-er,
Bm      Bm/A            E/G#  A
   For I know love will never die.
```

Refrain 2

```
A                  G
   Every little thing she does,
                 G/A  A* G/A   A*
She does for me,        yeah, ___
                        G
And you know the things she does,
                 G/A  A* G/A  A*
She does for me,        ooh. ___
```

Solo

```
| A      | D   E  | A      | G    D | Bm  Bm/A | E/G#  A ||
```

Refrain 3

```
A                  G
   Every little thing she does,
                 G/A  A* G/A   A*
She does for me,        yeah, ___
                        G
And you know the things she does,
                 G/A  A* G/A  A*
She does for me,        ooh. ___
```

Coda

```
|: A  D  E
              Every little thing. :|   Repeat to fade
```

For No One

Words & Music by John Lennon & Paul McCartney

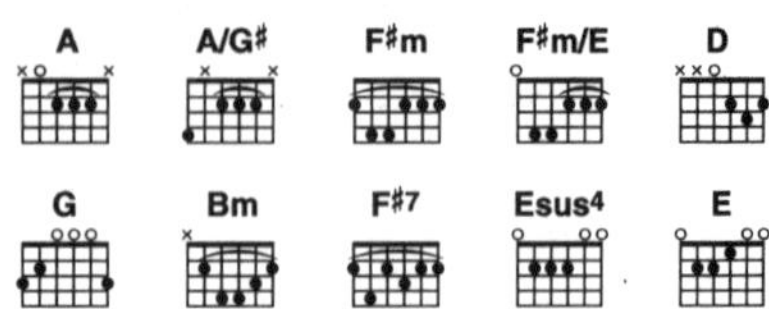

Kapo zweiter Bund

```
              A                    A/G♯
Strophe 1       Your day breaks,   your mind aches,
              F♯m                F♯m/E
                You find that all her words
                  D               G
              Of kindness linger on
                             A
              When she no longer needs you.

              A                 A/G♯
Strophe 2       She wakes up,   she makes up,
              F♯m               F♯m/E
                She takes her time
                             D             G
              And doesn't feel she has to hurry,
                        A
              She no longer needs you.

                             Bm               F♯7
Refrain 1     And in her eyes you see nothing,
              Bm                                               F♯7
                No sign of love behind the tears cried for no-one,
              Bm                                          Esus4   E
                A love that should have lasted years.
```

Strophe 3

```
A                 A/G#
  You want her,   you need her,
F#m              F#m/E
  And yet, you don't believe her
D                   G
When she says her love is dead,
     A
You think she needs you.
```

Solo

```
| A  A/G# | F#m  F#m/E | D   G | A      ||
```

Refrain 2

```
             Bm            F#7
And in her eyes you see nothing,
Bm                                         F#7
  No sign of love behind the tears cried for no-one,
Bm                                    Esus4  E
  A love that should have lasted years.
```

Strophe 4

```
A                   A/G#
  You stay home,   she goes out,
F#m              F#m/E       D
  She says that long ago she knew someone,
     G
But now she's gone,
     A
She doesn't need him.
```

Strophe 5

```
A                    A/G#
  Your day breaks,   your mind aches,
F#m              F#m/E          D
  There will be times when all the things she said
     G
Will fill your head,
A
You won't forget her.
```

Refrain 3

```
             Bm            F#7
And in her eyes you see nothing,
Bm                                         F#7
  No sign of love behind the tears cried for no-one,
Bm                                    Esus4  E
  A love that should have lasted years.
```

From Me To You

Words & Music by John Lennon & Paul McCartney

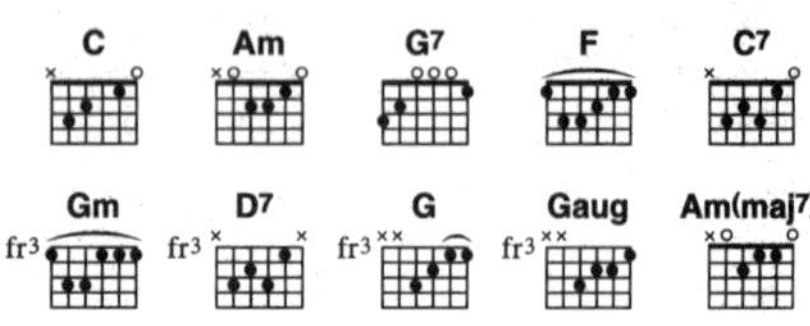


```
               C                     Am
Intro          Da da da da-da dum dum da,
               C                     Am
               Da da da da-da dum dum da.

                       C                  Am
Strophe 1      If there's anything that you want,
                       C                G7
               If there's anything I can do,
                    F                 Am
               Just call on me and I'll send it along,
                    C        G7   C     Am
               With love from me to you.

                       C                    Am
Strophe 2      I've got everything that you want,
                    C                G7
               Like a heart that's oh so true,
                    F                Am
               Just call on me and I'll send it along,
                    C        G7   C     C7
               With love from me to you.

                     Gm               C
Bridge 1       I got arms that long to hold you,
                     F
               And keep you by my side,
                     D7
               I got lips that long to kiss you,
                     G           Gaug
               And keep you satisfied.
```

Strophe 3

```
              C                  Am
If there's anything that you want,
              C               G7
If there's anything I can do,
     F                   Am
Just call on me and I'll send it along,
      C          G7    C      Am
With love from me to you.
```

Solo

```
| C      | Am     From me.

| C      | G7     To you.
     F                   Am
Just call on me and I'll send it along,
      C          G7    C      C7
With love from me to you.
```

Bridge 2

```
     Gm                  C
I got arms that long to hold you,
     F
And keep you by my side,
     D7
I got lips that long to kiss you,
     G               Gaug
And keep you satisfied.
```

Strophe 4

```
              C                  Am
If there's anything that you want,
              C               G7
If there's anything I can do,
     F                   Am
Just call on me and I'll send it along,
      C          G7    C
With love from me to you.
   Am
To you,
   Am(maj7)
To you,
   C     Am
To you.
```

Get Back

Words & Music by John Lennon & Paul McCartney

A5 G D/A D A7 D7

Intro | A5 | A5 | A5 | A5 G D/A ||

Strophe 1

```
A5
Jojo was a man who thought he was a loner
D                     A5
But he knew it couldn't last.

Jojo left his home in Tucson, Arizona
D                  A5
For some California grass.
```

Refrain 1

```
     A7
Get back, get back,
     D7                          A5        G  D/A
Get back to where you once belonged.
     A7
Get back, get back,
     D7                          A5
Get back to where you once belonged.

Get back Jojo.
```

Solo |: (A5) | A5 | D | A5 G D/A :|

Refrain 2

```
     A7
Get back, get back,
     D7                          A5        G  D/A
Get back to where you once belonged.
     A7
Get back, get back,
     A5                          D
Get back to where you once belonged.
          A5
Get back Jo.
```

Solo 𝄆 (A5) | A5 | D | A5 G D/A 𝄇

Strophe 2

```
A5
Sweet Loretta Martin thought she was a woman
D                       A5
But she was another man.

All the girls around her say she's got it coming
D                            A5
But she gets it while she can.
```

Refrain 3

```
    A7
Get back, get back,
    D7                            A5        G   D/A
Get back to where you once belonged.
    A7
Get back, get back,
    D7                            A5
Get back to where you once belonged.

Get back Loretta.
```

Solo 𝄆 A5 | A5 | D | A5 G D/A 𝄇

Refrain 4

```
    A7
Get back, get back,
    D7                            A5        G   D/A
Get back to where you once belonged.
    A7
Get back, get back,
    D7                            D
Get back to where you once belonged.   Ooh.

𝄆 A5        | A5        | D        | A5   G   D/A 𝄇   Repeat to fade
             Get back.
```

Girl

Words & Music by John Lennon & Paul McCartney

Kapo achter Bund

Strophe 1

```
             Em            B7            Em    Em7
Is there anybody going to listen to my story,
Am                                  G      B7
All about the girl who came to stay?
               Em                B7                   Em              Em7
She's the kind of girl you want so much it makes you sorry,
Am                                 Em
Still, you don't regret a single day.
```

Refrain 1

```
     G     Bm  Am  D7
Ah, girl ______
G    Bm   Am  D7
Girl, girl.
```

Strophe 2

```
             Em               B7                Em          Em7
When I think of all the times I've tried so hard to leave her,
Am                                   G     B7
She will turn to me and start to cry.
              Em           B7                Em  Em7
And she promises the earth to me and I be-lieve her,
Am                                     Em
After all this time, I don't know why.
```

Refrain 2

```
     G     Bm  Am  D7
Ah, girl ______
G    Bm   Am  D7
Girl, girl.
```

```
               Am
Bridge         She's the kind of girl
                           E
               Who puts you down when friends are there,
                          Am   E
               You feel a fool.
               Am
               When you say she's looking good,
                   E
               She acts as if it's understood,
                     Am        C
               She's cool, ooh, ooh, ooh.

               G    Bm   Am  D7
Refrain 3      Girl ______
               G    Bm   Am  D7
               Girl, girl.

                       Em                B7                    Em        Em7
Strophe 3      Was she told when she was young that pain would lead to pleasure?
               Am                        G       B7
               Did she understand it when they said,
                      Em                   B7            Em       Em7
               That a man must break his back to earn his day of leisure?
               Am                            Em
               Will she still believe it when he's  dead?

                   G    Bm   Am  D7
Refrain 4      Ah, girl ______
               G    Bm   Am  D7
               Girl, girl.

Solo           | Em  B7 | Em  Em7 | Am     | G  B7  |

               | Em  B7 | Em  Em7 | Am     | Em     ||

                   G    Bm   Am  D7
Refrain 5      Ah, girl ______
               G    Bm   Am  D7
               Girl, girl.          Fade out
```

Give Peace A Chance

Words & Music by John Lennon & Paul McCartney

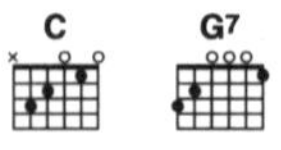

Kapo erster Bund

```
              N.C.
Intro         Two, one, two , three, four.

              | C      | C      | C      | C      ||

              C
Strophe 1     Ev'rybody's talking about

              Bagism, Shagism,

              Dragism, Madism,

              Ragism, Tagism,

              Thisism, Thatism.

              Isn't it the most?

              C          G7
Refrain 1     All we are saying,
                             C
              Is give peace a chance.
                         G7
              All we are saying,
                           C
              Is give peace a chance.
```

Strophe 2

C
Ev'rybody's talking about
Ministers, Sinisters,
Banisters and Canisters,
Bishops and Fishops and
Rabbis and Popeyes,
Bye bye bye byes.

Refrain 2

Wie Refrain 1

Strophe 3

C
Ev'rybody's talking about
Revolution, Evolution,
Mastication, Flagelation,
Regulations, Integrations,
Meditations, United Nations,
Congratulations.

Refrain 3

Wie Refrain 1

Strophe 4

C
Ev'rybody's talking about
John and Yoko, Timmy Leary,
Rosemary, Tommy Smothers,
Bobby Dylan, Tommy Cooper,
Derek Taylor, Norman Mailer,
Alan Ginsberg, Hare Krishna, Hare, Hare Krishna.

Refrain 4

𝄆 Wie Refrain 1 𝄇 *Play 6 times*

Good Day Sunshine

Words & Music by John Lennon & Paul McCartney

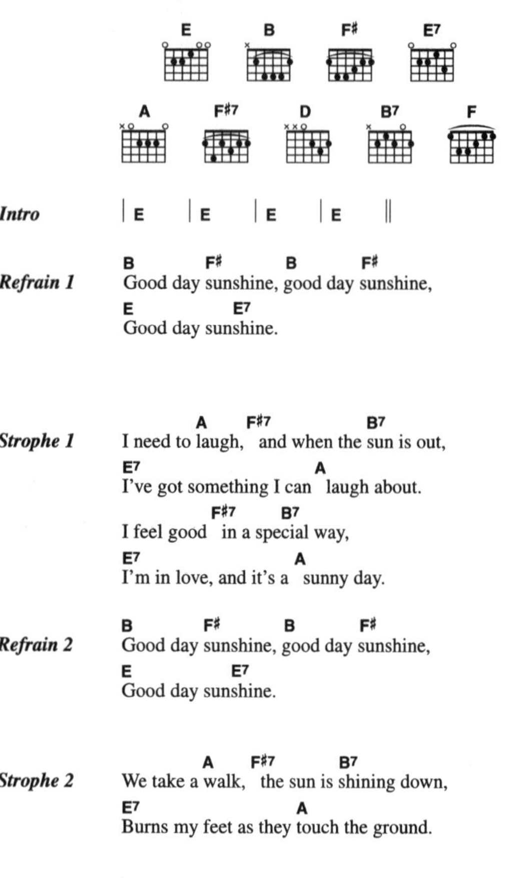

Intro | E | E | E | E ||

Refrain 1

```
B            F♯          B          F♯
Good day sunshine, good day sunshine,
E                 E7
Good day sunshine.
```

Strophe 1

```
                     A         F♯7                  B7
I need to laugh,   and when the sun is out,
E7                                        A
I've got something I can   laugh about.
                    F♯7         B7
I feel good   in a special way,
E7                                A
I'm in love, and it's a   sunny day.
```

Refrain 2

```
B            F♯          B          F♯
Good day sunshine, good day sunshine,
E                 E7
Good day sunshine.
```

Strophe 2

```
                       A        F♯7              B7
We take a walk,   the sun is shining down,
E7                                    A
Burns my feet as they touch the ground.
```

Solo | D B7 | E7 | A7 | D ||

Refrain 3

B F♯ B F♯
Good day sunshine, good day sunshine,
E E7
Good day sunshine.

Strophe 3

A F♯7 B7
Then we lie beneath a shady tree,
E7 A
I love her and she's loving me.
F♯7 B7
She feels good, she knows she's looking fine,
E7 A
I'm so proud to know that she is mine.

Refrain 4

B F♯ B F♯
Good day sunshine, good day sunshine,
E E7
Good day sunshine.

Refrain 5

B F♯ B F♯
Good day sunshine, good day sunshine,
E E7
Good day sunshine.
F
𝄆 Good day, sunshine. 𝄇 *Repeat to fade*

Good Morning, Good Morning

Words & Music by John Lennon & Paul McCartney

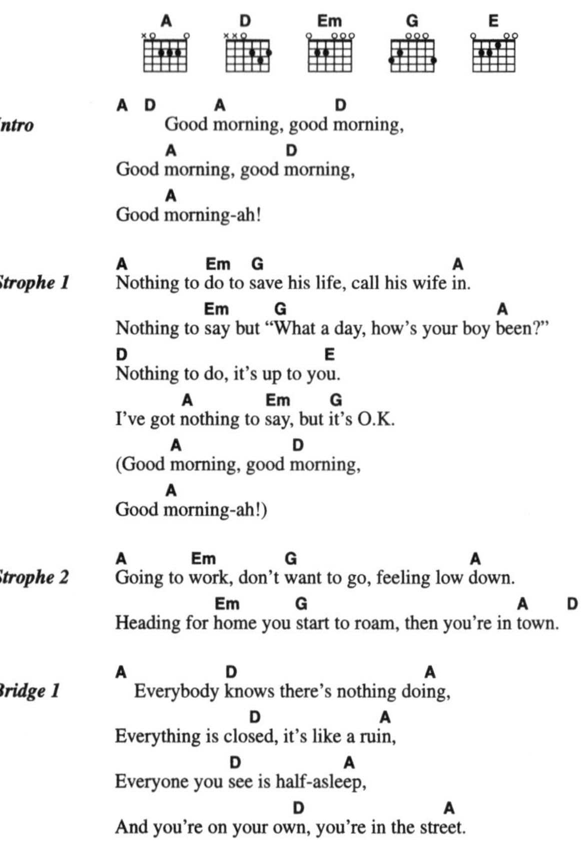

Intro

A D A D
Good morning, good morning,
A D
Good morning, good morning,
A
Good morning-ah!

Strophe 1

A Em G A
Nothing to do to save his life, call his wife in.
Em G A
Nothing to say but "What a day, how's your boy been?"
D E
Nothing to do, it's up to you.
A Em G
I've got nothing to say, but it's O.K.
A D
(Good morning, good morning,
A
Good morning-ah!)

Strophe 2

A Em G A
Going to work, don't want to go, feeling low down.
Em G A D
Heading for home you start to roam, then you're in town.

Bridge 1

A D A
Everybody knows there's nothing doing,
D A
Everything is closed, it's like a ruin,
D A
Everyone you see is half-asleep,
D A
And you're on your own, you're in the street.

Strophe 3

```
A       Em        G                             A
After a while you start to smile, now you feel cool.
           Em       G                       A
Then you decide to take a walk by the old school.
D                                   E
Nothing has changed, it's still the same,
         A           Em       G
I've got nothing to say, but it's O.K.
      A             D
(Good morning, good morning,
     A
Good morning-ah!)
```

Solo

```
| A Em G | G  A | A Em G | G  A | A  D ||
```

Bridge 2

```
A                       D           A
  People running round, it's five o'clock,
              D               A
Everywhere in town is getting dark,
             D              A
Everyone you see is full of life,
              D                A
It's time for tea and meet the wife.
```

Strophe 4

```
A        Em       G                             A
Somebody needs to know the time, glad that I'm here.
             Em          G                             A
Watching the skirt, you start to flirt, now you're in gear
D                          E
Go to a show, you hope she goes,
         A           Em       G
I've got nothing to say, but it's O.K.
      A             D        A
(Good morning, good morning, good!)
         A              D       A     D
|: (Good morning, good morning, good!)     :|   Repeat to fade
```

Got To Get You Into My Life

Words & Music by John Lennon & Paul McCartney

Intro | (G) | (G) | (G) | (G) ||

Strophe 1

G
I was alone, I took a ride,
F/G
I didn't know what I would find there.
G
Another road where maybe I
F/G
Could see another kind of mind there.

Bridge 1

Bm Bm(maj7) Bm7 Bm/G#
Ooh, then I suddenly see you,
Bm Bm(maj7) Bm7 Bm/G#
Ooh, did I tell you I need you
C C/B Am7 D7 G
Every single day of my life?

Strophe 2

G
You didn't run, you didn't lie,
F/G
You knew I wanted just to hold you.
G
And had you gone, you knew in time
F/G
We'd meet again, for I had told you.

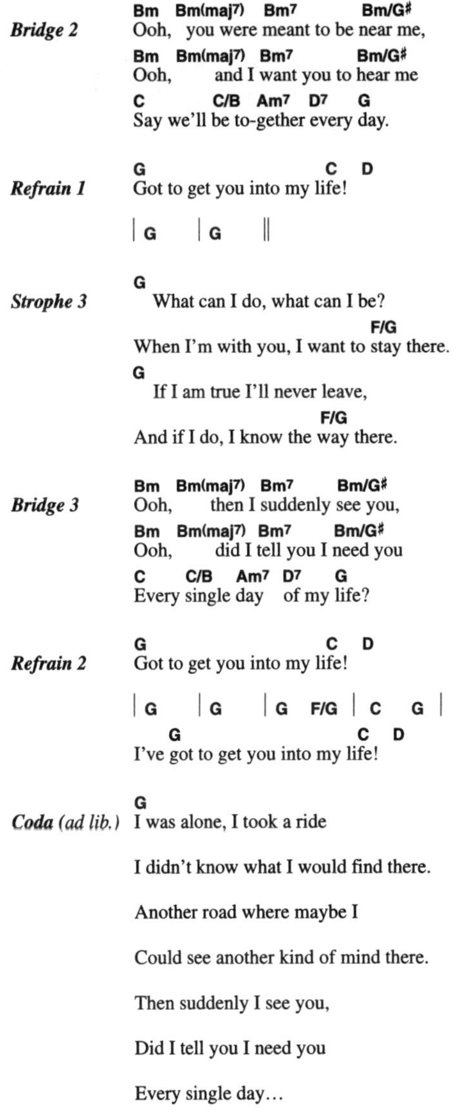

Bridge 2

Bm Bm(maj7) Bm7 Bm/G♯
Ooh, you were meant to be near me,
Bm Bm(maj7) Bm7 Bm/G♯
Ooh, and I want you to hear me
C C/B Am7 D7 G
Say we'll be to-gether every day.

Refrain 1

G C D
Got to get you into my life!

| G | G ||

Strophe 3

G
What can I do, what can I be?
F/G
When I'm with you, I want to stay there.
G
If I am true I'll never leave,
F/G
And if I do, I know the way there.

Bridge 3

Bm Bm(maj7) Bm7 Bm/G♯
Ooh, then I suddenly see you,
Bm Bm(maj7) Bm7 Bm/G♯
Ooh, did I tell you I need you
C C/B Am7 D7 G
Every single day of my life?

Refrain 2

G C D
Got to get you into my life!

| G | G | G F/G | C G |

G C D
I've got to get you into my life!

Coda (ad lib.)

G
I was alone, I took a ride

I didn't know what I would find there.

Another road where maybe I

Could see another kind of mind there.

Then suddenly I see you,

Did I tell you I need you

Every single day…

Happiness Is A Warm Gun

Words & Music by John Lennon & Paul McCartney

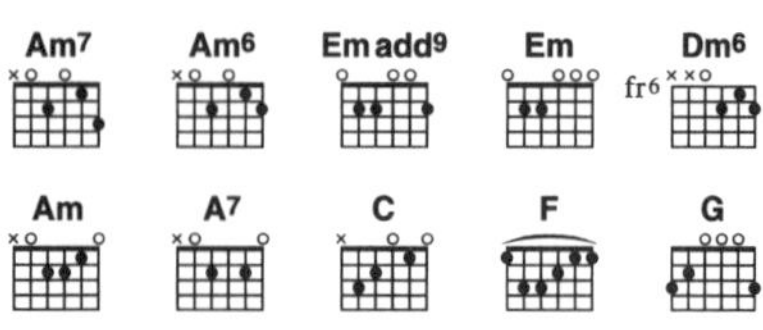

Intro

```
         Am7  Am6       Emadd9       Em
She's not a girl who misses much.
Am7                   Am6  Emadd9   Em
   Do-do-do-do-do-do,      oh yeah.
```

Strophe 1

```
Dm6
   She's well acquainted with the touch

Of the velvet hand,
                     Am
Like a lizard on a window pane.
    Dm6
The man in the crowd,
                                        Am
With the multicoloured mirrors on his hobnail boots.
Dm6
Lying with his eyes,
                                   Am
While his hands are busy working overtime.
Dm6
   A soap impression of his wife, which he ate,
                      Am
And donated to the National Trust.
```

```
| A7        | A7        | C    Am   ||
```

Strophe 2

```
A7
I need a fix, 'cause I'm going down,

Down to the bits that I left uptown,
C                       Am
I need a fix, 'cause I'm going down.
```

Strophe 3

```
   A7             C
|: Mother Superior, jump the gun,
A7                G
Mother Superior, jump the gun.  :|  Play 3 times
```

Strophe 4

```
  C       Am      F
{  Happiness is a warm gun,  G          C
{                          (Bang, bang, shoot, shoot.)

       Am     F               G
{Happiness is a warm gun, momma.       C
{                      (Bang, bang, shoot, shoot.)

        Am      F     G
When I hold you   in my arms,
C        Am     F       G
   And I feel my finger on your trigger,
C   Am      F             G
   I know nobody can do me no harm,
C
Because

       Am     F               G
{Happiness is a warm gun, momma.                 C
{                              (Bang, bang, shoot, shoot,)

  C       Am     F               G
{  Happiness is a warm gun, yes it is.       Fm
{                           (Bang, bang, shoot, shoot)

                        N.C.
Happiness is a warm, yes it is…

        C
{Gun. ____        Am   F     G     Well don't you know that
{          (Happiness… bang, bang, shoot, shoot)

C           Am        F            G        C
{Happiness            is a warm gun, momma.
{     (Happiness…                  is a warm gun,yeah!)
```

Hello Goodbye

Words & Music by John Lennon & Paul McCartney

Strophe 1

F6 C
You say yes, I say no,
G7 Am G7
You stay stop, but I say go, go, go.
Am G7
Oh no.
G G7 F/G
You say goodbye and I say;

Refrain 1

C C/B Am Asus2/G
Hello, hello, hello,
F A♭
I don't know why you say goodbye, I say hello,
C C/B Am Asus2/G
Hello, hello, hello,
F B♭9 C
I don't know why you say goodbye, I say hello.

Strophe 2

F6 C
I say high, you say low,
G7 Am G7
You say why and I say I don't know.
Am G7
Oh no.
G G7 F/G
You say goodbye and I say hello.

Refrain 2

C C/B Am
(Hello, goodbye, hello, goodbye,)
Hello, hello,

Asus2/G
(Hello, goodbye.) F A♭ C
I don't know why you say goodbye, I say hello.

C C/B Am
(Hello, goodbye, hello, goodbye,)
Hello, hello,

Asus2/G
(Hello, goodbye,) F B♭9 C
I don't know why you say goodbye, I say hello.
(Hello, goodbye.)

Bridge

F6 C G7
Why, why, why, why, why, why,

Am G7
Do you say goodbye, goodbye?

Am G7
Oh no.

G G7 F/G
You say goodbye and I say;

Refrain 3

Wie Refrain 1

Strophe 3

F6 C
You say yes, I say no,
(I say yes, but I may mean no,)

G7 Am G7
You say stop, but I say go, go, go.
(I can stay till it's time to go)

Am G7
Oh, no.

G G7 F/G
You say goodbye and I say;

Refrain 4

Wie Refrain 1

Refrain 5

C/B Am Asus2/G
Hello, hello,

F A♭ A♭ A♭/G A♭/G♭ F
I don't know why you say goodbye, I say hello, ________

C
Hello.

Coda

C
𝄆 Hela, heba, helloa. 𝄇 *Repeat to fade*

Helter Skelter

Words & Music by John Lennon & Paul McCartney

E7* E6 Eaug G E A E7

Intro | E7* ||

Strophe 1

```
   E7*                                              E6
When I get to the bottom I go back to the top of the slide.
                                    Eaug
Where I stop and I turn and I go for a ride,
                                     G
Till I get to the bottom, and I see you again,
          E
Yeah, yeah, yeah!
```

Strophe 2

```
E
Do you, don't you want me to love you?

I'm coming down fast, but I'm miles above you.

Tell me, tell me, tell me,
        G
Come on, tell me the answer,
         A                           E
Well, you may be a lover, but you ain't no dancer.
```

Refrain 1

```
A             E
Helter Skelter, Helter Skelter,
A             E
Helter Skelter, yeah!
```

| E | E ||

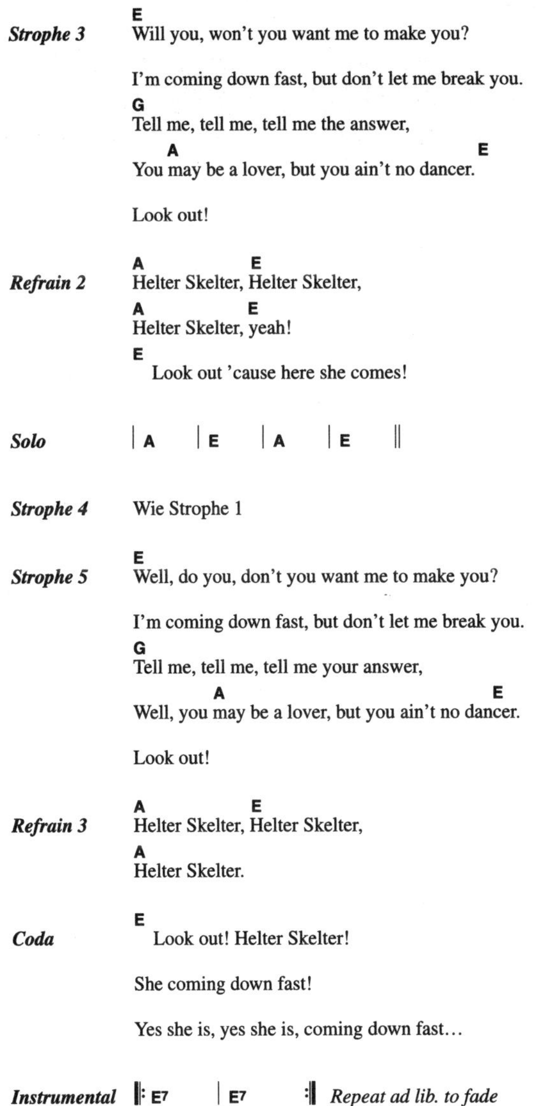

```
                 E
Strophe 3        Will you, won't you want me to make you?

                 I'm coming down fast, but don't let me break you.
                 G
                 Tell me, tell me, tell me the answer,
                     A                                  E
                 You may be a lover, but you ain't no dancer.

                 Look out!

                 A            E
Refrain 2        Helter Skelter, Helter Skelter,
                 A            E
                 Helter Skelter, yeah!
                 E
                   Look out 'cause here she comes!


Solo             | A     | E     | A     | E     ||


Strophe 4        Wie Strophe 1

                 E
Strophe 5        Well, do you, don't you want me to make you?

                 I'm coming down fast, but don't let me break you.
                 G
                 Tell me, tell me, tell me your answer,
                         A                                  E
                 Well, you may be a lover, but you ain't no dancer.

                 Look out!

                 A            E
Refrain 3        Helter Skelter, Helter Skelter,
                 A
                 Helter Skelter.

                 E
Coda               Look out! Helter Skelter!

                 She coming down fast!

                 Yes she is, yes she is, coming down fast…

Instrumental     |: E7     | E7     :|  Repeat ad lib. to fade
```

Here, There And Everywhere

Words & Music by John Lennon & Paul McCartney

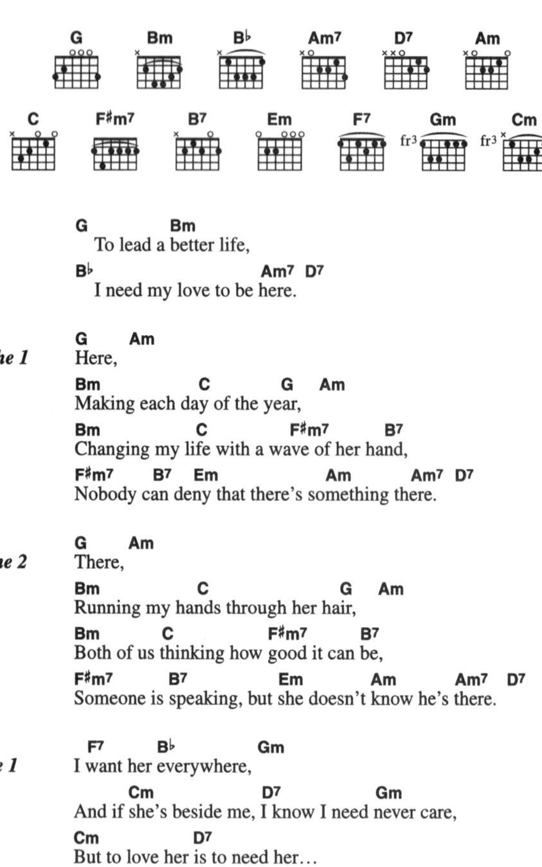

Intro

G Bm
To lead a better life,
B♭ Am7 D7
I need my love to be here.

Strophe 1

G Am
Here,
Bm C G Am
Making each day of the year,
Bm C F♯m7 B7
Changing my life with a wave of her hand,
F♯m7 B7 Em Am Am7 D7
Nobody can deny that there's something there.

Strophe 2

G Am
There,
Bm C G Am
Running my hands through her hair,
Bm C F♯m7 B7
Both of us thinking how good it can be,
F♯m7 B7 Em Am Am7 D7
Someone is speaking, but she doesn't know he's there.

Bridge 1

F7 B♭ Gm
I want her everywhere,
Cm D7 Gm
And if she's beside me, I know I need never care,
Cm D7
But to love her is to need her…

Strophe 3

G Am
Everywhere.

Bm C G Am
Knowing that love is to share,

Bm C F♯m7 B7
Each one believing that love never dies,

F♯m7 B7 Em Am Am7 D7
Watching their eyes and hoping I'm always there.

Bridge 2

F7 B♭ Gm
I want her everywhere,

Cm D7 Gm
And if she's beside me, I know I need never care,

Cm D7
But to love her is to need her…

Strophe 4

G Am
Everywhere.

Bm C G Am
Knowing that love is to share,

Bm C F♯m7 B7
Each one believing that love never dies,

F♯m7 B7 Em Am Am7 D7
Watching their eyes and hoping I'm always there.

Coda

G Am
I will be there

Bm C
And everywhere,

G Am Bm C G
Here, there and everywhere. ___

Hey Jude

Words & Music by John Lennon & Paul McCartney

E B7 A E7 A/G# A/F# A/E D

Kapo erster Bund

```
              E                         B7
*Strophe 1*   Hey Jude, don't make it bad,
                                           E
              Take a sad song and make it better.
                 A                               E
              Remember to let her into your heart,
                                  B7                    E
              Then you can start to make it better.

               (E)                  B7
*Strophe 2*   Hey Jude, don't be afraid,
                                                E
              You were made to go out and get her.
                  A                                   E
              The minute you let her under your skin,
                                B7                E    E7
              Then you begin to make it better.

                                             A
*Bridge 1*    And anytime you feel the pain,
                   A/G#     A/F#
              Hey Jude, refrain,
                          A/E       B7                   E           E7
              Don't carry the world upon your shoulders.
                                                A
              For well you know that it's a fool
                        A/G#    A/F#
              Who plays it cool
                     A/E          B7              E
              By making his world a little colder.
                          E7      B7
              Na na na na na, na na na na.
```

Strophe 3

E B7
Hey Jude, don't let me down,
E
You have found her, now go and get her.
A E
Remember to let her into your heart,
B7 E E7
Then you can start to make it better.

Bridge 2

A
So let it out and let it in,
A/G♯ A/F♯
Hey Jude, begin,
A/E B7 E E7
You're waiting for someone to perform with.
A
And don't you know that it's just you,
A/G♯ A/F♯
Hey Jude, you'll do,
A/E B7 E
The movement you need is on your shoulder.
E7 B7
Na na na na na, na na na na. Yeah.

Strophe 4

E B7
Hey Jude, don't make it bad,
E
Take a sad song and make it better.
A E
Remember to let her under your skin,
B7 E
Then you begin to make it better,

Better, better, better, better, better, oh.

Outro

E D
𝄆 Na ___ na na, na na na na, ___
A E
Na na na na. ___ Hey Jude. 𝄇 *Repeat to fade*

Honey Pie

Words & Music by John Lennon & Paul McCartney

Em A6 Am/D Cm G A7 D7

E♭7 E7 F♯ F C♯m7♭5 G7 Am

Intro

Em A6 Am/D
She was a working girl.
Cm G
North of England way.
Em A6 Am/D Cm G
Now she's hit the big time in the U. S. A.
A7
And if she could only hear me,
D7
This is what I'd say:

Strophe 1

G E♭7
Honey Pie, you are making me crazy,
E7 A7
I'm in love, but I'm lazy,
D7 G E♭7 D7
So won't you please come home?

Strophe 2

G E♭7
Oh, Honey Pie, my position is tragic,
E7 A7
Come and show me the magic
D7 G F♯ F
Of your Hollywood song.

Bridge 1

Em C♯m7♭5 G
You became a legend of the silver screen,
G7 C
And now the thought of meeting you
E7 Am D7
Makes me weak in the knee.

Strophe 3

```
   G                                   E♭7
Oh, Honey Pie, you are driving me frantic,
E7                 A7
   Sail across the Atlantic
D7                     G
   To be where you belong.
         E♭7       D7    G
Honey pie, come back to me.
```

Solo

```
| G   | G   | E♭7 | E7  | A7  | D7  ||
(me.)
G                E♭7  D7
   (I like it like that)
```

Strophe 4

```
G                                    E♭7
   …I like this kind of, hot kind of music,
E7
Hot kind of music,
A7
Play it to me,
D7                            G       F♯  F
Play it to me, Hollywood blues.
```

Bridge 2

```
Em                  C♯m7♭5          G           G7
Will the wind that blew her boat across the sea
C                   E7               Am  D7
   Kindly send her sailing back to me.
```

Strophe 5

```
    G                                   E♭7
Now, Honey pie, you are making me crazy,
E7                  A7
   I'm in love, but I'm lazy,
D7                      G
   So won't you please come home?
                     E♭7        D7     G
(Come, come back to me Honey Pie,) ____

| G   | E♭7 | E7  | A7  |
D7                G
(Honey Pie, Honey Pie.)

| E♭7  D7 | G   ||
```

I Am The Walrus

Words & Music by John Lennon & Paul McCartney

B A A6 G F F6 E

E7 D D7 A/G C Dadd9/F♯ B7 Dsus4

Intro | B | B A A6 | G F F6 | E | E7 | D | D7 ||

Strophe 1

A A/G
I am he as you are he

C D A A/G
As you are me and we are all together.

C
See how they run like pigs from a gun,

D A
See how they fly, I'm crying.

Strophe 2

A A/G Dadd9/F♯
Sitting on a cornflake,

F G A A/G
Waiting for the van to come.

F
Corporation T-shirt stupid bloody Tuesday,

B7
Man, you been a naughty boy, you let your face grow long.

Refrain 1

C D
I am the eggman, they are the eggmen,

E
I am the walrus,

Goo goo g'joob.

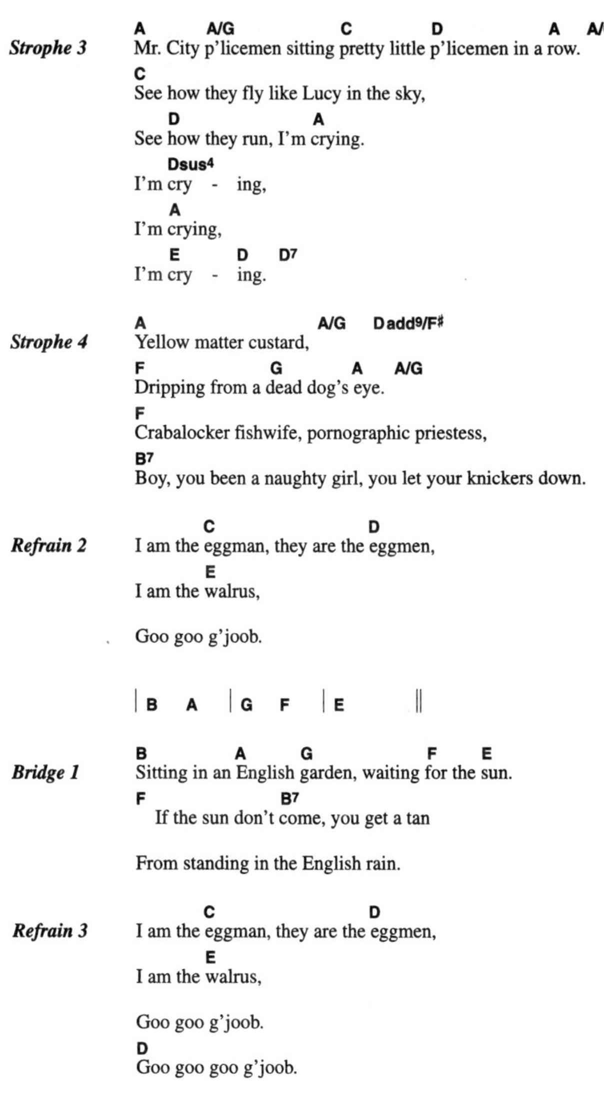

```
              A        A/G                C          D                A    A/G
*Strophe 3*   Mr. City p'licemen sitting pretty little p'licemen in a row.
              C
              See how they fly like Lucy in the sky,
                  D                 A
              See how they run, I'm crying.
                 Dsus4
              I'm cry  -  ing,
                 A
              I'm crying,
                 E        D   D7
              I'm cry  -  ing.
```

```
              A                            A/G     Dadd9/F#
*Strophe 4*   Yellow matter custard,
              F                G          A    A/G
              Dripping from a dead dog's eye.
              F
              Crabalocker fishwife, pornographic priestess,
              B7
              Boy, you been a naughty girl, you let your knickers down.
```

```
                          C                    D
*Refrain 2*   I am the eggman, they are the eggmen,
                          E
              I am the walrus,

              Goo goo g'joob.
```

```
              | B   A  | G   F  | E       ||
```

```
              B          A      G                F     E
*Bridge 1*    Sitting in an English garden, waiting for the sun.
              F                  B7
                 If the sun don't come, you get a tan

              From standing in the English rain.
```

```
                          C                    D
*Refrain 3*   I am the eggman, they are the eggmen,
                          E
              I am the walrus,

              Goo goo g'joob.
              D
              Goo goo goo g'joob.
```

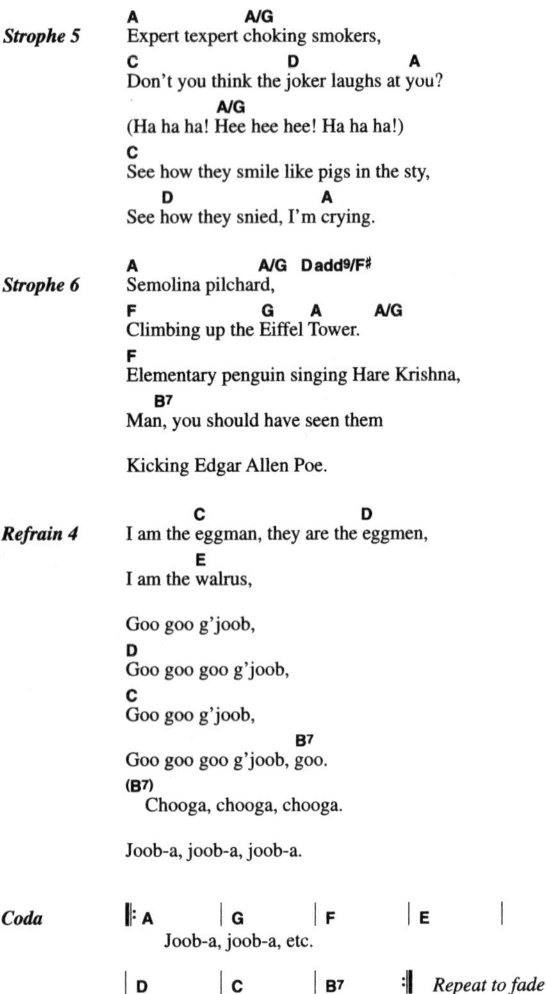

Strophe 5

A A/G
Expert texpert choking smokers,
C D A
Don't you think the joker laughs at you?
A/G
(Ha ha ha! Hee hee hee! Ha ha ha!)
C
See how they smile like pigs in the sty,
D A
See how they snied, I'm crying.

Strophe 6

A A/G Dadd9/F#
Semolina pilchard,
F G A A/G
Climbing up the Eiffel Tower.
F
Elementary penguin singing Hare Krishna,
B7
Man, you should have seen them

Kicking Edgar Allen Poe.

Refrain 4

C D
I am the eggman, they are the eggmen,
E
I am the walrus,

Goo goo g'joob,
D
Goo goo goo g'joob,
C
Goo goo g'joob,
B7
Goo goo goo g'joob, goo.
(B7)
Chooga, chooga, chooga.

Joob-a, joob-a, joob-a.

Coda

|: A | G | F | E |
Joob-a, joob-a, etc.

| D | C | B7 :| *Repeat to fade*

I Feel Fine

Words & Music by John Lennon & Paul McCartney

D7 C7 G7 G Bm C Am

Intro | (D7) | (D7) | (C7) | (C7) |
Feedback
| (G7) | (G7) | (G7) | (G7) ||

Strophe 1
G7
Baby's good to me, you know,

She's happy as can be, you know
D7
She said so.
C7 G7
I'm in love with her and I feel fine.

Strophe 2
G7
Baby says she's mine, you know,

She tells me all the time, you know
D7
She said so.
C7 G7
I'm in love with her and I feel fine.

Bridge 1
G Bm
I'm so glad
C D7
That she's my little girl,
G Bm
She's so glad,
Am D7
She's telling all the world;

Strophe 3

G7
That her baby buys her things, you know,

He buys her diamond rings, you know

D7
She said so.

C7 G7
She's in love with me and I feel fine.

Solo

| G7 | G7 | G7 | G7 | D7 | D7 ||

| (D7) | (D7) | (C7) | (C7) |

| (G7) | (G7) | (G7) | (G7) ||

Strophe 4

G7
Baby says she's mine, you know,

She tells me all the time, you know

D7
She said so.

C7 G7
I'm in love with her and I feel fine.

Bridge 2

G Bm
I'm so glad

C D7
That she's my little girl,

G Bm
She's so glad,

Am D7
She's telling all the world;

Strophe 5

G7
That her baby buys her things, you know,

He buys her diamond rings, you know

D7
She said so.

C7 G7
She's in love with me and I feel fine.

Coda

D7 C7 G7
She's in love with me and I feel fine.

||: G7 | G7 | G7 | G7 :|| *Repeat to fade*

I Saw Her Standing There

Words & Music by John Lennon & Paul McCartney

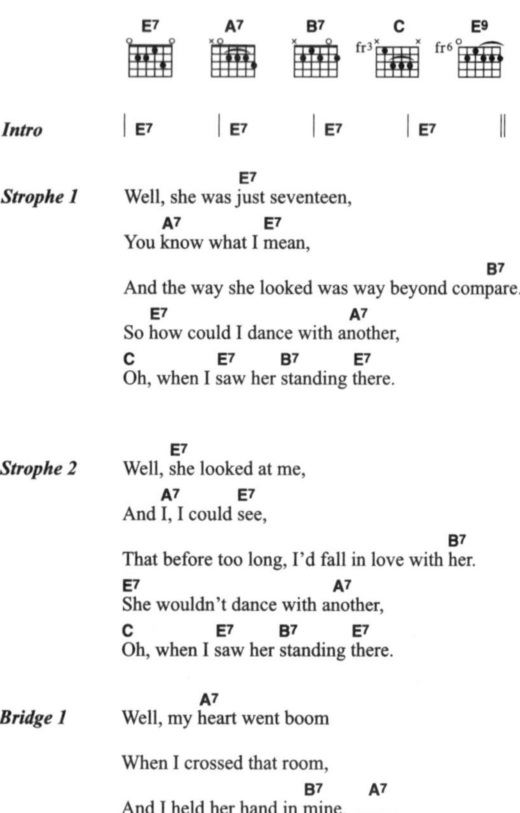

Intro | E7 | E7 | E7 | E7 ||

Strophe 1

```
                 E7
Well, she was just seventeen,
     A7            E7
You know what I mean,
                                                     B7
And the way she looked was way beyond compare.
   E7                                  A7
So how could I dance with another,
C              E7          B7          E7
Oh, when I saw her standing there.
```

Strophe 2

```
          E7
Well, she looked at me,
       A7          E7
And I, I could see,
                                                B7
That before too long, I'd fall in love with her.
E7                                   A7
She wouldn't dance with another,
C              E7          B7          E7
Oh, when I saw her standing there.
```

Bridge 1

```
                A7
Well, my heart went boom

When I crossed that room,
                              B7        A7
And I held her hand in mine. _____
```

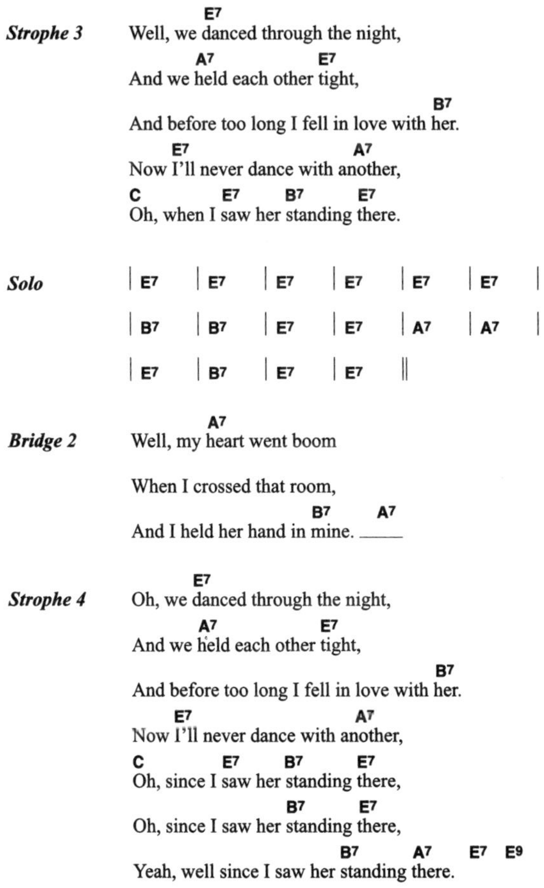

Strophe 3

E7
Well, we danced through the night,
A7 E7
And we held each other tight,
B7
And before too long I fell in love with her.
E7 A7
Now I'll never dance with another,
C E7 B7 E7
Oh, when I saw her standing there.

Solo

| E7 | E7 | E7 | E7 | E7 | E7 |
| B7 | B7 | E7 | E7 | A7 | A7 |
| E7 | B7 | E7 | E7 ||

Bridge 2

A7
Well, my heart went boom
When I crossed that room,
B7 A7
And I held her hand in mine. ____

Strophe 4

E7
Oh, we danced through the night,
A7 E7
And we held each other tight,
B7
And before too long I fell in love with her.
E7 A7
Now I'll never dance with another,
C E7 B7 E7
Oh, since I saw her standing there,
B7 E7
Oh, since I saw her standing there,
B7 A7 E7 E9
Yeah, well since I saw her standing there.

I Should Have Known Better

Words & Music by John Lennon & Paul McCartney

G D Em C B7 G7

```
Intro        | G   D | G   D | G   D | G   D ||

             G D G D                  G           D      G    D
Strophe 1    I ______ should have known better with a girl like you,
                       G          D               Em
             That I would love everything that you do,
                    C           D          G  D  G
             And I do, hey hey hey, and I do.

             D           G D G D           G             D          G   D
Strophe 2    Woh woh, I ______ never realised what a kiss could be,
                         G    D             Em
             This could only happen to me.
                          C              B7
             Can't you see, can't you see?

             Em                C              G              B7
Bridge 1       That when I tell you that I love you, oh,
             Em                                       G       G7
               You're gonna say you love me too, __ oh,
             C                   D               G       Em
               And when I ask you to be mine __
             C                        D                 G     D    G
               You're gonna say you love me too.

             D       G D G D                   G              D         G    D
Strophe 3    So, oh, I ______ should have realised a lot of things before.
                         G                          D          Em
             If this is love, you've got to give me more,
                               C                D              G       D  G  D
             Give me more, hey hey hey, give me more.
```

Solo
G D	G D	G D	G D
G D	Em	C	D	
G D	G D	
Woh woh,
Strophe 4
G D G D G D G D
I ___ never realised what a kiss could be,
G D Em
This could only happen to me.
C B7
Can't you see, can't you see?
Bridge 2
Em C G B7
That when I tell you that I love you, oh,
Em G G7
You're gonna say you love me too, ___ oh,
C D G Em
And when I ask you to be mine ___
C D G D G
You're gonna say you love me too.
Outro
D G D G
You love me too.
D G D G
: You love me too. :
Repeat to fade

I Wanna Be Your Man

Words & Music by John Lennon & Paul McCartney

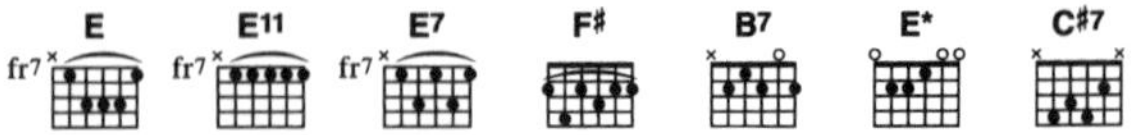

E E11 E7 F♯ B7 E* C♯7

Strophe 1

E E11 E E11
I wanna be your lover, baby,
E E11 E E11
I wanna be your man,
E E11 E E11
I wanna be your lover, baby,
E E11 E7
I wanna be your man.

Strophe 2

E E11 E E11
Love you like no other, baby,
E E11 E E11
Like no other can,
E E11 E E11
Love you like no other, baby,
E E11 E7
Like no other can.

Refrain 1

N.C. F♯7 B7
I wanna be your man,
E* C♯7
I wanna be your man,
F♯7 B7
I wanna be your man,
E E11
I wanna be your ma - an.

Strophe 3

E E11 E E11
Tell me that you love me, baby,
E E11 E E11
Let me understand,
E E11 E E11
Tell me that you love me, baby,
E E11 E7
I wanna be your man.

Strophe 4

```
E          E11       E      E11
I wanna be your lover, baby,
E          E11       E     E11
I wanna be your man,
E          E11       E      E11
I wanna be your lover, baby,
E          E11       E7
I wanna be your man.
```

Refrain 2

```
N.C.                 F#7    B7
I wanna be your man,
                     E*     C#7
I wanna be your man,
                     F#7    B7
I wanna be your man,
                     E      E11
I wanna be your ma  -  an.
```

Solo

```
|: E   E11 | E   E11 | E   E11 | E   E11 :|
```

Play 3 times

Strophe 5

```
E          E11       E      E11
I wanna be your lover, baby,
E          E11       E     E11
I wanna be your man,
E          E11       E      E11
I wanna be your lover, baby,
E          E11       E7
I wanna be your man.
```

Strophe 6

```
E             E11      E       E11
Love you like no other, baby,
E          E11  E        E11
Like no other can,
E             E11      E       E11
Love you like no other, baby,
E          E11  E7
Like no other can.
```

Refrain 3 Wie Refrain 2

Coda

```
|:  E  E11  E              E11       E
              I wanna be your man.  :|
```

Repeat to fade

I Want To Hold Your Hand

Words & Music by John Lennon & Paul McCartney

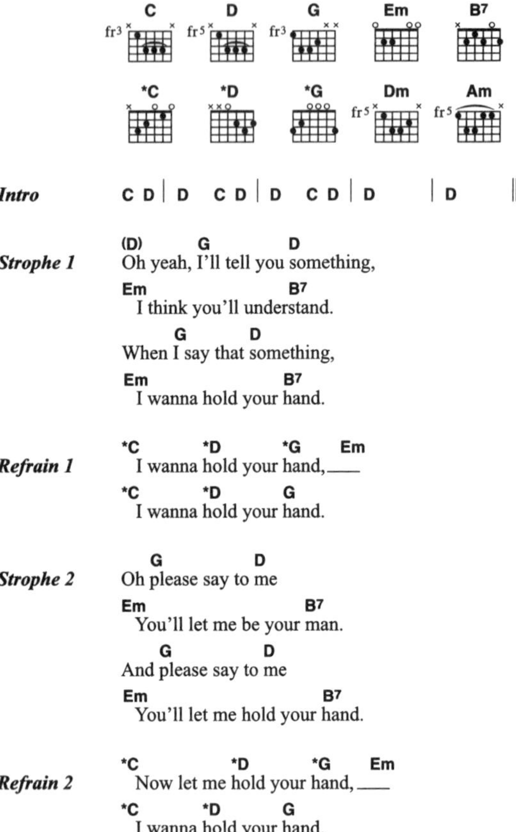

Intro C D | D C D | D C D | D | D ||

Strophe 1
```
(D)        G             D
Oh yeah, I'll tell you something,
Em                    B7
  I think you'll understand.
       G        D
When I say that something,
Em                  B7
  I wanna hold your hand.
```

Refrain 1
```
*C         *D          *G      Em
  I wanna hold your hand,___
*C         *D          G
  I wanna hold your hand.
```

Strophe 2
```
    G            D
Oh please say to me
Em                     B7
  You'll let me be your man.
     G              D
And please say to me
Em                          B7
  You'll let me hold your hand.
```

Refrain 2
```
*C              *D          *G      Em
  Now let me hold your hand,___
*C         *D          G
  I wanna hold your hand.
```

```
             Dm            G
Bridge 1       And when I touch you
                   C          Am
             I feel happy inside.
             Dm            G
               It's such a feeling
                         C             D
             That my love I can't hide,
             C       D     C       D
             I can't hide, I can't hide.

                   G                D
Strophe 3    Yeah, you got that something,
             Em                       B7
               I think you'll understand.
                    G            D
             When I say that something,
             Em                      B7
               I wanna hold your hand.

             *C          *D          *G     Em
Refrain 3      I wanna hold your hand, ___
             *C          *D          G
               I wanna hold your hand.

Bridge 2     Wie Bridge 1

                   G                D
Strophe 4    Yeah, you got that something,
             Em                       B7
               I think you'll understand.
                    G            D
             When I feel that something,
             Em                      B7
               I wanna hold your hand.

             *C          *D          *G     Em
Refrain 4      I wanna hold your hand, ___
             *C          *D          B7
               I wanna hold your hand,
             *C          *D          *C       *G
               I wanna hold your hand.
```

I Want To Tell You

Words & Music by John Lennon & Paul McCartney

A7 A7sus4 A B7 E7♭9 (fr6) Bm Bdim Asus4

Intro | A7 | A7sus4 | A7 | A7sus4 ||

```
              A
*Strophe 1*     I want to tell you,
                                   B7
              My head is filled with things to say.
              E7♭9
                 When you're here,
                                             A7
              All those words they seem to slip away.

              A
*Strophe 2*     When I get near you,
                                 B7
              The games begin to drag me down.
              E7♭9
                 It's alright,
                                            A7
              I'll make you maybe next time around.

              Bm           Bdim          A
*Bridge 1*      But if I seem to act unkind,
                         B7             Bm
              It's only me, it's not my mind,
              Bdim             A           Asus4
                 That is confusing things.
```

Strophe 3

A
I want to tell you,
B7
I feel hung up and I don't know why.
E7♭9
I don't mind, I could wait forever,
A7
I've got time.

Bridge 2

Bm Bdim A
Sometimes I wish I knew you well,
B7 Bm
Then I could speak my mind and tell you,
Bdim A Asus4
Maybe you'd understand.

Strophe 4

A
I want to tell you,
B7
I feel hung up and I don't know why.
E7♭9
I don't mind, I could wait forever,
A7
I've got time, ______

I've got time, ______

I've got time. ______ *Fade out*

I Will

Words & Music by John Lennon & Paul McCartney

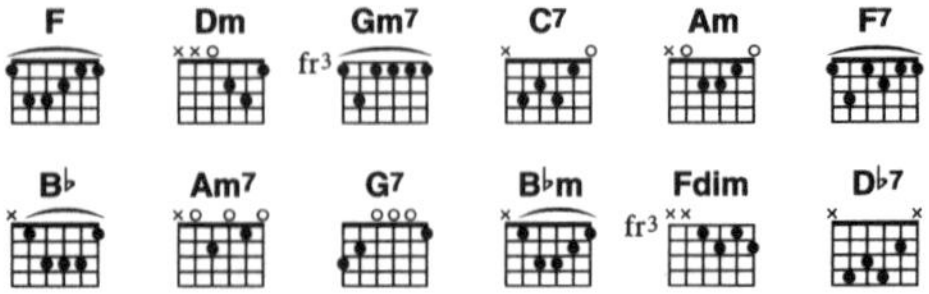

F Dm Gm7 C7 Am F7

B♭ Am7 G7 B♭m Fdim D♭7

Strophe 1

F Dm Gm7 C7
Who knows how long I've loved you?
F Dm Am
You know I love you still,
F7 B♭ C7 Dm F
Will I wait a lonely lifetime?
B♭ C7 F Dm Gm7 C7
If you want me to, I will.

Strophe 2

F Dm Gm7 C7
For if I ever saw you,
F Dm Am
I didn't catch your name.
F7 B♭ C7 Dm F
But it never really mattered
B♭ C7 F F7
I will always feel the same.

Bridge

B♭ Am7 Dm
Love you forever and forever,
Gm7 C7 F F7
Love you with all my heart,
B♭ Am7 Dm
Love you whenever we're together,
G7 C7
Love you when we're apart.

```
                  F          Dm   Gm7       C7
*Strophe 3*   And when at last I find you,
                   F          Dm      Am
              Your song will fill the air.
              F7     B♭       C7   Dm        B♭m  F
              Sing it loud so I can hear you,
                        B♭   C7   Dm        B♭m  F
              Make it easy to be near you,
                        B♭        C7
              For the things you do
                 Dm  B♭m  F    Fdim
              Endear you   to me
              Gm7     C7        D♭7
              Oh, you know I will,
                   F    F7
              I will. ___
```

```
Coda          | B♭  Am | Dm       | Gm7  C7 | F          ||
                Ooo, __________       la. _______
```

If I Fell

Words & Music by John Lennon & Paul McCartney

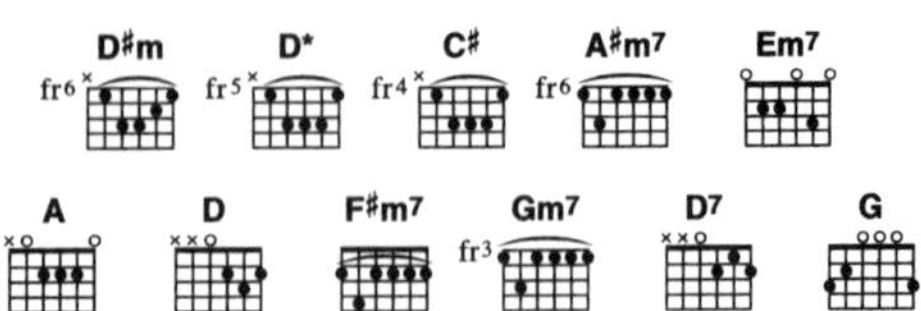

Intro

D♯m
If I fell in love with you,
D*
Would you promise to be true
C♯ A♯m7
And help me understand?
D♯m
'Cause I've been in love before,
D*
And I found that love was more
Em7 A
Than just holding hands.

Strophe 1

D Em7 F♯m7 Em7
If I give my heart to you,
A
I must be sure
D Em7 F♯m7 Em7
From the ve-ry start, that you
A D Gm7 A
Would love me more than her.

Strophe 2

D Em7 F♯m7 Em7
If I trust in you, oh please,
A
Don't run and hide.
D Em7 F♯m7 Em7
If I love you too, oh please
A D7
Don't hurt my pride like her.

Bridge 1

```
(D7)                           G
'Cause I couldn't stand the pain
      Gm7                              D
And I, would be sad if our new love
         A
Was in vain.
```

Strophe 3

```
     D     Em7 F#m7    Em7
So I hope you  see that I
         A
Would love to love you,
D     Em7  F#m7     Em7
And that   she will cry
        A                  D7
When she learns we are two.
```

Bridge 2

```
(D7)                           G
'Cause I couldn't stand the pain
      Gm7                              D
And I, would be sad if our new love
         A
Was in vain.
```

Strophe 4

```
     D     Em7 F#m7    Em7
So I hope you  see that I
         A
Would love to love you,
D     Em7  F#m7     Em7
And that   she will cry
        A                  D
When she learns we are two.
    Gm7               D      Gm7  D
If I fell in love with you.
```

I'll Follow The Sun

Words & Music by John Lennon & Paul McCartney

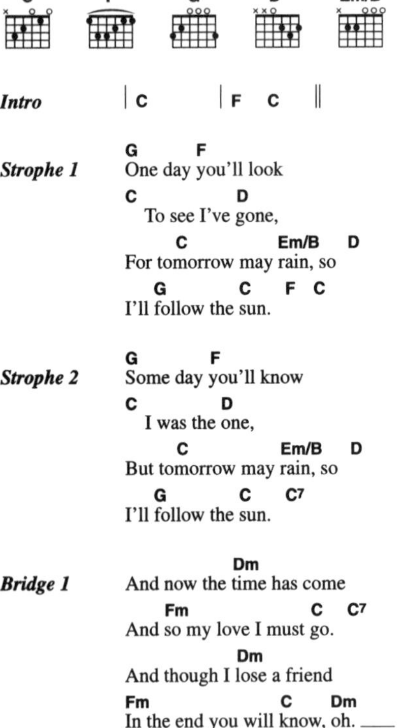

Intro | C | F C ||

Strophe 1

```
G        F
One day you'll look
C          D
   To see I've gone,
        C           Em/B   D
For tomorrow may rain, so
    G         C    F   C
I'll follow the sun.
```

Strophe 2

```
G         F
Some day you'll know
C         D
   I was the one,
        C           Em/B   D
But tomorrow may rain, so
    G         C    C7
I'll follow the sun.
```

Bridge 1

```
                 Dm
And now the time has come
      Fm               C   C7
And so my love I must go.
                 Dm
And though I lose a friend
Fm               C      Dm
In the end you will know, oh. ___
```

Strophe 3

```
G        F
One day you'll find
C           D
  That I have gone,
     C          Em/B  D
But tomorrow may rain, so
   G        C    F  C
I'll follow the sun.
```

Solo

```
| G       | F       | C       | D       ||
     C          Em/B  D
Yes, tomorrow may rain, so
   G        C    C7
I'll follow the sun.
```

Bridge 2

```
           Dm
And now the time has come
    Fm              C   C7
And so my love I must go.
           Dm
And though I lose a friend
Fm            C     Dm
In the end you will know, oh. ___
```

Strophe 4

```
G        F
One day you'll find
C           D
  That I have gone,
     C          Em/B  D
But tomorrow may rain, so
   G        C    F  C
I'll follow the sun.
```

I'll Get You

Words & Music by John Lennon & Paul McCartney

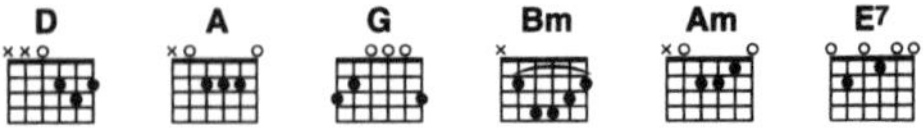

D A G Bm Am E7

Intro

    D   A
Oh yeah, oh yeah,
    D   A
Oh yeah, oh yeah.

Strophe 1

 D
Imagine I'm in love with you,
   G   A
It's easy 'cause I know.
      D   Bm
I've imagined I'm in love with you
G   A
Many, many, many times before.
        D   Am
It's not like me to pretend,
        D   Bm
But I'll get you, I'll get you in the end,
      G   A
Yes I will, I'll get you in the end,
    D   A
Oh yeah, oh yeah.

Strophe 2

  D
I think about you night and day,
  G   A
I need you and it's true,
        D   Bm
When I think about you, I can say,
     G   A
I'm never, never, never, never blue.
        D   Am
So I'm telling you, my friend,
         D   Bm
That I'll get you, I'll get you in the end,

cont.

```
      G                          A
Yes I will, I'll get you in the end,
   D       A
Oh yeah, oh yeah.
```

Bridge 1

```
                G
Well there's gonna be a time,
              D
When I'm gonna change your mind,
         E7                              A
So you might as well resign yourself to me,

Oh yeah.
```

Strophe 3

```
 D
Imagine I'm in love with you,
   G           A
It's easy 'cause I know.
     D              Bm
I've imagined I'm in love with you
G                            A
Many, many, many times before.
       D          Am
It's not like me to pretend,
       D                              Bm
But I'll get you, I'll get you in the end,
      G                          A
Yes I will, I'll get you in the end,
   D       A
Oh yeah, oh yeah,
   D       A       D
Oh yeah, oh yeah, oh yeah.
```

I'm Happy Just To Dance With You

Words & Music by John Lennon & Paul McCartney

Intro | C♯m | F♯m G♯ | C♯m | F♯m G♯ ‖

Refrain 1

```
                C#m
Before this dance is through,
            F#m       G#
I think I'll love you too,
         A6                  B6           E6    B7
I'm so happy when you dance with me.
```

Strophe 1

```
         E                G#m        F#m     B
I don't wanna kiss or hold your hand,
        E               G#m  F#m    B
If it's funny, try and understand.
           A                F#m                 E*   C#m
There is really nothing else I'd rather do,
              A                Baug          E        B7
'Cause I'm happy just to dance with you.
```

Strophe 2

```
         E                G#m        F#m     B
I don't need to hug or hold you tight,
        E                  G#m      F#m     B
I just wanna dance with you all night.
       A                       F#m                   E*   C#m
In this world there's nothing I would rather do,
              A                Baug          E
'Cause I'm happy just to dance with you.
```

Bridge 1

C♯m F♯m G♯
Just to dance with you
C♯m F♯m G♯
Is everything I need.
C♯m
Before this dance is through,
F♯m G♯
I think I'll love you too,
A6 B6 E6 B7
I'm so happy when you dance with me.

Strophe 3

E G♯m F♯m B
If somebody tries to take my place,
E G♯m F♯m B
Let's pretend we just can't see his face.
A F♯m E* C♯m
In this world there's nothing I would rather do,
A Baug E
'Cause I'm happy just to dance with you.

Bridge 2

Wie Bridge 1

Strophe 4

E G♯m F♯m B
If somebody tries to take my place,
E G♯m F♯m B
Let's pretend we just can't see his face.
A F♯m E C♯m
In this world there's nothing I would rather do,
A Baug C♯m
I've discovered I'm in love with you.
F♯m G♯
Oh - oh,
A Baug C♯m
'Cause I'm happy just to dance with you.
F♯m G♯
Oh - oh,
A6 B6
Oh - oh,
E6
Oh!

I'm So Tired

Words & Music by John Lennon & Paul McCartney

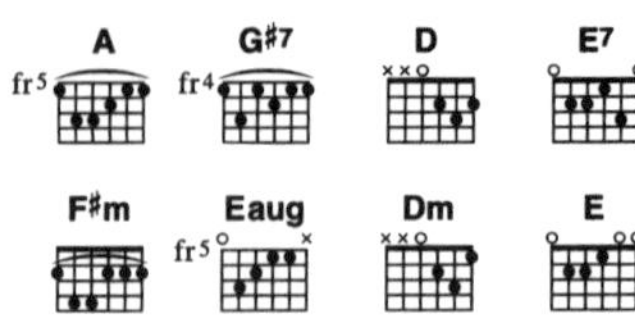

Strophe 1

A G♯7 D E7
I'm so tired, I haven't slept a wink,
A F♯m D E7
I'm so tired, my mind is on the blink.
A Eaug
I wonder should I get up
F♯m Dm
And fix myself a drink?

No, no, no.

Strophe 2

A G♯7 D E7
I'm so tired, I don't know what to do,
A F♯m D E7
I'm so tired, my mind is set on you.
A Eaug
I wonder should I call you,
F♯m Dm
But I know what you would do.

Refrain 1

A
You'd say I'm putting you on,

But it's no joke, it's doing me harm,
E
You know I can't sleep, I can't stop my brain,

You know it's three weeks, I'm going insane,
D
You know I'd give you everything I've got
A
For a little peace of mind.

Strophe 3

```
    A  G#7      D            E7
I'm so tired, I'm feeling so upset,
  A      F#m          D                E7
Although  I'm so tired,  I'll have another cigarette,
    A                Eaug
And  curse Sir Walter Raleigh,
        F#m        Dm
He was such a stupid get.
```

Refrain 2

```
A
You'd say I'm putting you on,

But it's no joke, it's doing me harm,
          E
You know I can't sleep, I can't stop my brain,

You know it's three weeks, I'm going insane,
             D
You know I'd give you everything I've got
                         A
For a little peace of mind.
```

Coda

```
   D
I'd give you everything I've got
                         A
For a little peace of mind.
   D
I'd give you everything I've got
                         A
For a little peace of mind
```

In My Life

Words & Music by John Lennon & Paul McCartney

A E F♯m A7/G

D Dm G B Dm7

Intro | A | E | A | E ||

Strophe 1

```
                A      E   F♯m     A7/G
There are places I remember
          D    Dm          A
All my life, ___ though some have changed,
          A     E        F♯m    A7/G
Some forever, not for better,
              D      Dm      A
Some have gone ___ and some remain.
```

Bridge 1

```
              F♯m               D
All these places had their moments,
     G                        A
With lovers and friends I still can recall,
              F♯m              B
Some are dead and some are living,
   Dm7          A
In my life I've loved them all.
```

| A | E ||

Strophe 2

```
          A         E              F♯m      A7/G
But of all these friends and lovers,
              D  Dm        A
There is no-one compares with you,
              A          E          F♯m        A7/G
And these memories lose their meaning
             D         Dm      A
When I think of love as something new.
```

Bridge 2

```
              F♯m                    D
Though I know I'll never lose affection
   G                       A
For people and things that went before,
 F♯m                             B
I know I'll often stop and think about them,
  Dm7       A
In my __ life I love you more.
```

Solo

```
‖: A   E   | F♯m  A7/G | D   Dm  | A      :‖
```

Bridge 3

```
              F♯m                    D
Though I know I'll never lose affection
   G                       A
For people and things that went before,
 F♯m                             B
I know I'll often stop and think about them,
  Dm7       A
In my __ life I love you more.
```

Coda

```
| A    | E    | Dm7       N.C.      A
               In my __ life I love you more.

| E    | A    ‖
```

It Won't Be Long

Words & Music by John Lennon & Paul McCartney

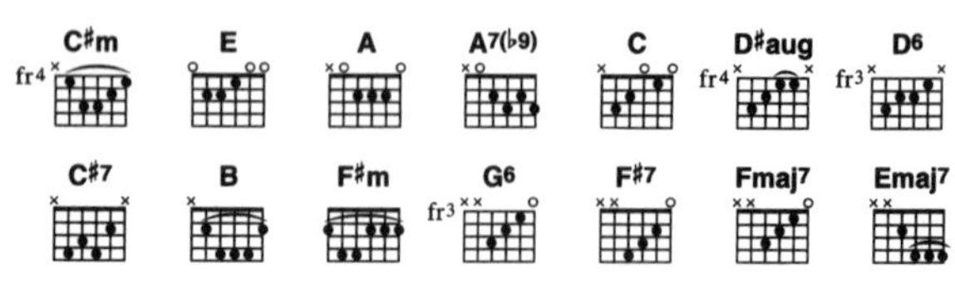

Refrain 1

C♯m
It won't be long, yeah, yeah, yeah,
E
It won't be long, yeah, yeah, yeah,
C♯m
It won't be long, yeah,
A A7(♭9) E
Till I belong to you.

Strophe 1

(E) C E
Every night when everybody has fun,
C E
Here am I sitting all on my own.

Refrain 2

Wie Refrain 1

Bridge 1

E D♯aug
Since you left me I'm so alone,
D6 C♯7
Now you're coming, you're coming on home,
A B
I'll be good like I know I should,
F♯m B
You're coming home, you're coming home.

Strophe 2

E C E
Every night the tears come down from my eyes,
C E
Every day I've done nothing but cry.

Refrain 3

C♯m
It won't be long, yeah, yeah, yeah,
E
It won't be long, yeah, yeah, yeah,
C♯m
It won't be long, yeah,
A A7(♭9) E
Till I belong to you.

Bridge 2

E D♯aug
Since you left me I'm so alone,
D6 C♯7
Now you're coming, you're coming on home,
A B
I'll be good like I know I should,
F♯m B
You're coming home, you're coming home.

Strophe 3

E C E
So, every day we'll be happy I know,
C E
Now I know that you won't leave me no more.

Refrain 4

C♯m
It won't be long, yeah, yeah, yeah,
E
It won't be long, yeah, yeah, yeah,
C♯m
It won't be long, yeah,
A N.C. G6 F♯7 Fmaj7 Emaj7
Till I belong to you. ________________

It's Only Love

Words & Music by John Lennon & Paul McCartney

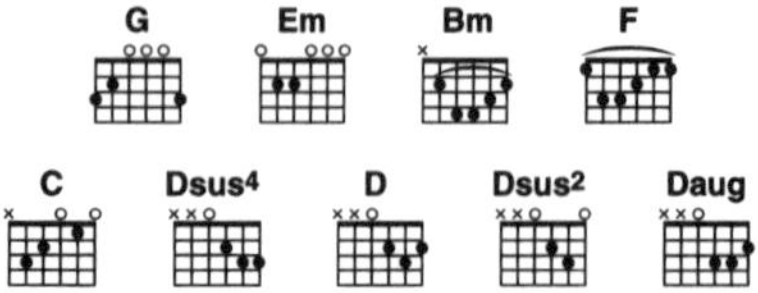

G Em Bm F

C Dsus4 D Dsus2 Daug

Kapo fünfter Bund

Intro | G | Em | G | Em ||

Strophe 1

```
G    Bm        F    C        Dsus4  D  Dsus2  D
I get high when I see you go by,
Daug
My oh my,
G         Bm      F    C         Dsus4  D  Dsus2  D
When you sigh my, my inside just flies,
Daug
Butterflies.
C             D                 G          Em
Why am I so shy when I'm beside you?
```

Refrain 1

```
           F                D
It's only love and that is all,
                G             Em
Why should I feel the way I do?
           F                D
It's only love and that is all,
             C           D
But it's so hard loving you. ______
```

Strophe 2

```
G    Bm        F          C          Dsus4  D  Dsus2  D
Is it right that you and I should fight
Daug
Every night?
G        Bm      F            C             Dsus4  D  Dsus2  D
Just the sight of you makes night time bright,
Daug
Very bright.
C              D                    G          Em
Haven't I the right to make it up, girl?
```

Refrain 2

```
          F                   D
It's only love and that is all,
                G                 Em
Why should I feel the way I do?
          F                   D
It's only love and that is all,
              C               D
But it's so hard loving you,
              C               D
Yes it's so hard loving you,
            G   Em  G    Em
Loving you. ________
```

Coda

```
| G      | Em      | G       ||
```

I've Just Seen A Face

Words & Music by John Lennon & Paul McCartney

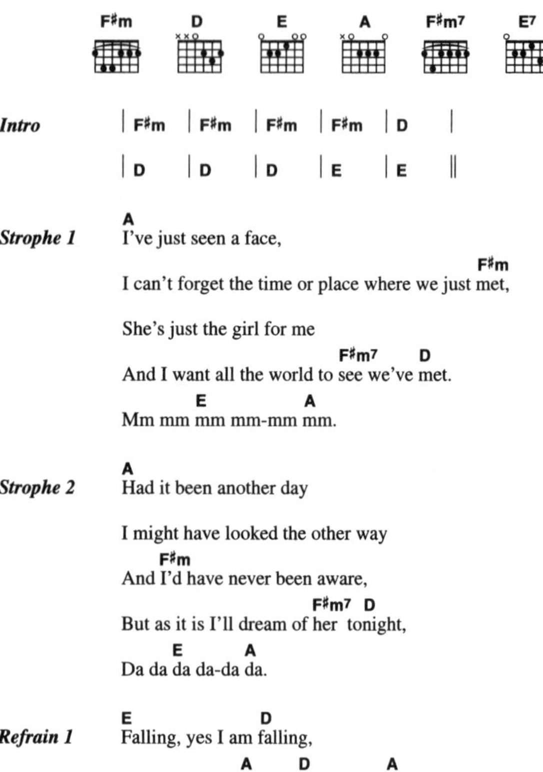

Intro | F♯m | F♯m | F♯m | F♯m | D |
| D | D | D | E | E ||

```
                A
Strophe 1       I've just seen a face,
                                                  F♯m
                I can't forget the time or place where we just met,

                She's just the girl for me
                                            F♯m7     D
                And I want all the world to see we've met.
                       E             A
                Mm mm mm mm-mm mm.

                A
Strophe 2       Had it been another day

                I might have looked the other way
                    F♯m
                And I'd have never been aware,
                                         F♯m7  D
                But as it is I'll dream of her  tonight,
                      E       A
                Da da da da-da da.

                E             D
Refrain 1       Falling, yes I am falling,
                              A      D         A
                And she keeps calling   me back again.
```

Strophe 3

```
A
I have never know the like of this,

I've been alone and I have
F♯m
Missed things and kept out of sight,
                                F♯m7      D
But other girls were never quite like this,
        E        A
Da da da da-da da.
```

Refrain 2

Wie Refrain 1

Solo

```
| A    | A    | A         | A    | F♯m  | F♯m  |
| F♯m  | F♯m F♯m7 | D     | D    | E    | A    ||
```

Refrain 3

```
E7                D
Falling, yes I am falling,
                   A        D          A
And she keeps calling   me back again.
```

Strophe 4

```
A
I've just seen a face,
                                                   F♯m
I can't forget the time or place where we just met,

She's just the girl for me
                                   F♯m7     D
And I want all the world to see we've met.
              E          A
Mm mm mm, da-da da.
```

Refrain 4

Wie Refrain 1

Refrain 5

Wie Refrain 1

Coda

```
     E                   D
Oh, falling, yes I am falling,
                   A        D                  E    A
And she keeps calling   me back again.
```

Julia

Words & Music by John Lennon & Paul McCartney

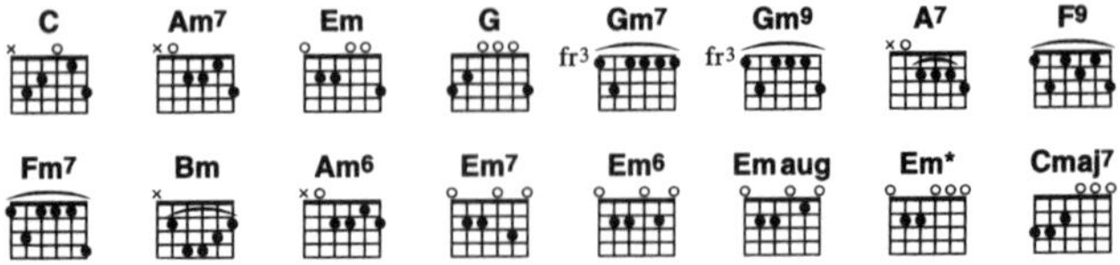

C Am7 Em G Gm7 Gm9 A7 F9

Fm7 Bm Am6 Em7 Em6 Em aug Em* Cmaj7

Kapo zweiter Bund

Refrain 1

C Am7 Em
Half of what I say is meaningless,
C Am7 Em G C
But I say it just to reach you, Ju - lia.

Strophe 1

C Am7 Gm7 Gm9 A7 F9 Fm7
Ju - lia, Ju - lia, ocean child, calls me,
C Am7 Em G C
So I sing a song of love, Ju - lia.

Strophe 2

C Am7 Gm7 Gm9 A7 F9 Fm7
Ju - lia, sea-shell eyes, windy smile, calls me,
C Am7 Em G C
So I sing a song of love, Ju - lia.

Bridge

Bm C
Her hair of floating sky is shimmering,
Am7 Am6
Glimmering
Em7 Em6 Em aug Em*
In the sun. ______

Strophe 3

C Am7 Gm7 Gm9 A7 F9 Fm7
Ju - lia, Ju - lia, morning moon, touch me,
C Am7 Em G C
So I sing a song of love, Ju - lia.

Refrain 2

C Am7 Em
When I cannot sing my heart,
C Am7 Em G C
I can only speak my mind, Ju - lia.

Strophe 4

C Am7 Gm7 Gm9 A7 F9 Fm7
Ju - lia, sleeping sand, silent cloud, touch me,
C Am7 Em G C Am7
So I sing a song of love, Ju - lia.

Coda

Gm7 Gm9 A7
Mm, ______
F9 Fm7
Calls me,
C Am7
So I sing a song of love
Em C
For Ju - lia,
Em C
Ju - lia,
Em G Cmaj7
Ju - lia.

Lady Madonna

Words & Music by John Lennon & Paul McCartney

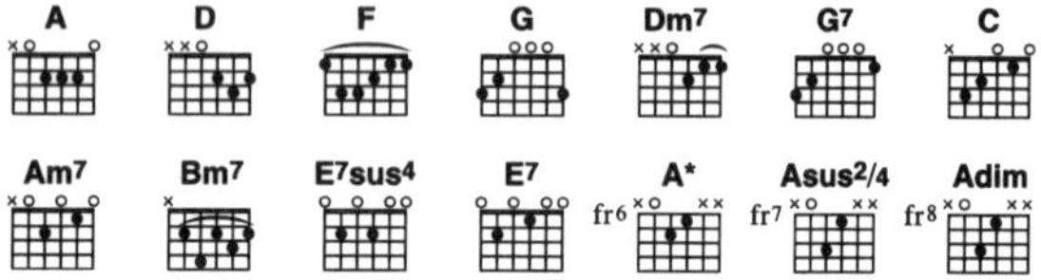

A D F G Dm7 G7 C

Am7 Bm7 E7sus4 E7 A* Asus2/4 Adim

fr6 fr7 fr8

Intro | A D | A D | A D | F G A ||

Strophe 1

```
A           D     A                D
Lady Madonna, children at your feet,
A                     D              F    G    A
Wonder how you manage to make ends meet.
                 D         A                   D
Who finds the money when you pay the rent?
A                        D           F    G    A
Did you think that money was heaven sent?
```

Bridge 1

```
Dm7                                     G7
Friday night arrives without a suitcase,
C                                      Am7
Sunday morning, creeping like a nun.
Dm7                                              G7
MondayÕs child has learned to tie his bootlace.
C    Bm7        E7sus4  E7
See how they run. _____
```

Strophe 2

```
A           D     A               D
Lady Madonna, baby at your breast,
A                     D            F   G   A
Wonder how you manage to feed the rest.
```

| A D | A D | A D | F G A ||

Solo

```
| Dm7   | G7    | C     | Am7   | Dm7   | G7    ||
C   Bm7     E7sus4  E7
See how they run. ____
```

Strophe 3

```
A        D     A            D
Lady Madonna, lying on the bed,
A              D            F    G    A
Listen to the music playing in your head.

| A  D  | A  D  | A  D  | F G A ||
```

Bridge 2

```
Dm7                          G7
Tuesday afternoon is never-ending,
C                                      Am7
Wednesday morning, papers didn't come.
Dm7                                          G7
Thursday night, your stockings needed mending:
C   Bm7     E7sus4  E7
See how they run. ____
```

Strophe 4

```
A        D     A              D
Lady Madonna, children at your feet,
A                   D            F      G     A*   Asus2/4   Adim   A*
Wonder how you manage to make ends meet. ____
```

Coda

```
| A*  Asus2/4 | Adim  Asus2/4  A ||
```

Let It Be

Words & Music by John Lennon & Paul McCartney

C G Am Fmaj7 F6 F C/G

Intro | C G | Am Fmaj7 F6 | C G | F C ||

Strophe 1

C G
When I find myself in times of trouble,
Am Fmaj7 F6
Mother Mary comes to me,
C G F C
Speaking words of wisdom, let it be.
C G
And in my hour of darkness
Am Fmaj7 F6
She is standing right in front of me,
C G F C
Speaking words of wisdom, let it be.

Refrain 1

Am C/G F C
Let it be, let it be, let it be, let it be,
G F C
Whisper words of wisdom, let it be.

Strophe 2

C G
And when the broken hearted people
Am Fmaj7 F6
Living in the world agree,
C G F C
There will be an answer, let it be.
C G
For though they may be parted there is
Am Fmaj7 F6
Still a chance that they will see.
C G F C
There will be an answer, let it be.

Refrain 2

Am C/G F C
Let it be, let it be, let it be, let it be,
G F C
There will be an answer, let it be.
Am C/G F C
Let it be, let it be, let it be, let it be,
G F C
Whisper words of wisdom, let it be.

| F C | G F C | F C | G F C |

Solo

|: C G | Am F | C G | F C :|

Refrain 3

Am C/G F C
Let it be, let it be, let it be, let it be,
G F C
Whisper words of wisdom, let it be.

Strophe 3

C G
And when the night is cloudy,
Am Fmaj7 F6
There is still a light that shines on me,
C G F C
Shine until tomorrow, let it be.
C G
I wake up to the sound of music,
Am Fmaj7 F6
Mother Mary comes to me,
C G F C
Speaking words of wisdom, let it be.

Refrain 4

Am C/G F C
Let it be, let it be, let it be, let it be,
G F C
There will be an answer, let it be.
Am C/G F C
Let it be, let it be, let it be, let it be,
G F C
There will be an answer, let it be.
Am C/G F C
Let it be, let it be, let it be, let it be,
G F C
Whisper words of wisdom, let it be.

| F C | G F C ||

Love Me Do

Words & Music by John Lennon & Paul McCartney

G C D

Intro | G | C | G | C | G | C | G | G ||

Refrain 1

```
G                C
Love, love me do,
      G             C
You know I love you.
    G          C
I'll always be true,

So please ___
N.C.      G      C    G             C
Love me do, ___ oh, love me do.
```

Refrain 2

```
G                C
Love, love me do,
      G             C
You know I love you.
    G          C
I'll always be true,

So please ___
N.C.      G      C    G             C
Love me do, ___ oh, love me do.
```

Bridge

```
D
Someone to love,
C             G
Somebody new.
D
Someone to love,
C                G
Someone like you.
```

Refrain 3

```
G                  C
Love, love me do,
     G                C
You know I love you.
    G             C
I'll always be true,

So please ___
N.C.        G      C    G
Love me do, ___ oh, love me do.
```

Solo

```
|: D      | D      | C      | G       :|
|  G      | G      | G      | G  (D)  ||
```

Refrain 4

```
G                  C
Love, love me do,
     G                C
You know I love you.
    G             C
I'll always be true,

So please ___
N.C.        G      C    G             C
Love me do, ___ oh, love me do.
          G           C
|: Yeah, love me do,
     G            C
Oh, love me do.        :|  Repeat to fade
```

Lovely Rita

Words & Music by John Lennon & Paul McCartney

B A E D B7

C#m F# G F#m Bsus4 Am

Gitarre einen Halbton tiefer stimmen

```
Intro         | B     | A     | E     | B     ||

              B          A
              Lovely Rita meter maid,
              E          B
              Lovely Rita meter maid.

              E          D    A
Refrain 1     Lovely Rita meter maid,
              E                    B7
              Nothing can come between us,
              C#m                  F#            B7
              When it gets dark, I tow your heart away.

              E             A
Strophe 1       Standing by a parking meter,
              D                 G
                When I caught a glimpse of Rita
              E                          B7
              Filling in a ticket in her little white book.

              E             A
Strophe 2       In a cap, she looked much older,
              D             G
                And the bag across her shoulder
              E                                 B7
              Made her look a little like a military man.

              | E  C#m  F#m  B ||
```

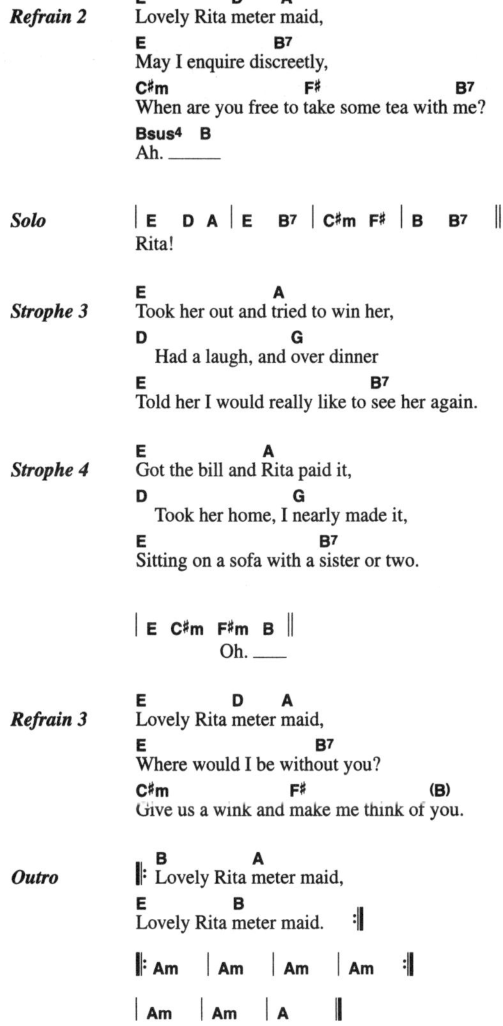
Refrain 2
E D A
Lovely Rita meter maid,
E B7
May I enquire discreetly,
C#m F# B7
When are you free to take some tea with me?
Bsus4 B
Ah. ______
Solo
| E D A | E B7 | C#m F# | B B7 ||
Rita!
Strophe 3
E A
Took her out and tried to win her,
D G
Had a laugh, and over dinner
E B7
Told her I would really like to see her again.
Strophe 4
E A
Got the bill and Rita paid it,
D G
Took her home, I nearly made it,
E B7
Sitting on a sofa with a sister or two.
| E C#m F#m B ||
Oh. ____
Refrain 3
E D A
Lovely Rita meter maid,
E B7
Where would I be without you?
C#m F# (B)
Give us a wink and make me think of you.
Outro
B A
||: Lovely Rita meter maid,
E B
Lovely Rita meter maid. :||
||: Am | Am | Am | Am :||
| Am | Am | A ||

Lucy In The Sky With Diamonds

Words & Music by John Lennon & Paul McCartney

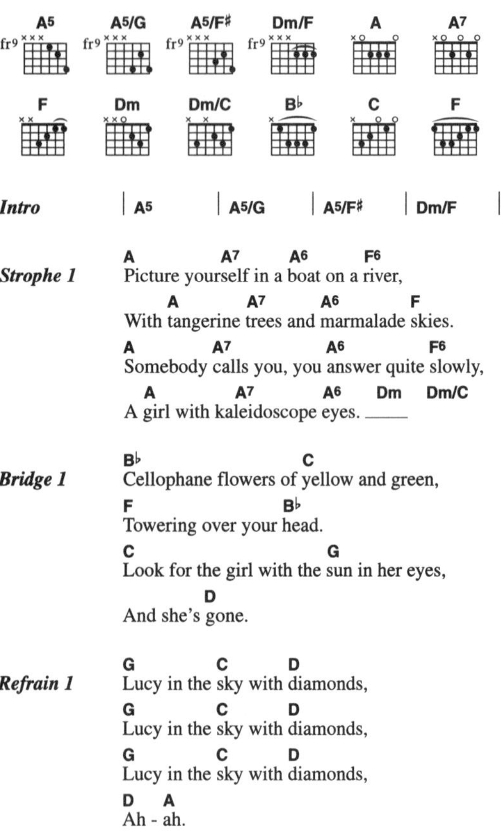

Intro | A5 | A5/G | A5/F♯ | Dm/F ||

Strophe 1

A A7 A6 F6
Picture yourself in a boat on a river,

A A7 A6 F
With tangerine trees and marmalade skies.

A A7 A6 F6
Somebody calls you, you answer quite slowly,

A A7 A6 Dm Dm/C
A girl with kaleidoscope eyes. ____

Bridge 1

B♭ C
Cellophane flowers of yellow and green,

F B♭
Towering over your head.

C G
Look for the girl with the sun in her eyes,

D
And she's gone.

Refrain 1

G C D
Lucy in the sky with diamonds,

G C D
Lucy in the sky with diamonds,

G C D
Lucy in the sky with diamonds,

D A
Ah - ah.

Strophe 2

```
(A)            A7          A6            F6
Follow her down to a bridge by a fountain,
        A                  A7          A6            F
Where rocking horse people eat marshmallow pies.
A           A7             A6            F6
Everyone smiles as you drift past the flowers,
     A          A7        A6     Dm    Dm/C
That grow so incredibly high. ___
```

Bridge 2

```
Bb                    C
Newspaper taxis appear on the shore,
F                      Bb
Waiting to take you away.
C                               G
Climb in the back with your head in the clouds,
               D
And you're gone.
```

Refrain 2

```
G           C        D
Lucy in the sky with diamonds,
G           C        D
Lucy in the sky with diamonds,
G           C        D
Lucy in the sky with diamonds,
D    A
Ah - ah.
```

Strophe 3

```
(A)            A7         A6        F6
Picture yourself on a train in a station,
      A          A7             A6           F
With plasticine porters with looking glass ties.
A           A7          A6           F6
Suddenly someone is there at the turnstile,
     A              A7          A6     Dm
The girl with kaleidoscope eyes. ___
```

Refrain 3

```
   G           C        D
|: Lucy in the sky with diamonds,
G           C        D
Lucy in the sky with diamonds,
G           C        D
Lucy in the sky with diamonds,
D    A
Ah - ah.     :|   Repeat to fade
```

Magical Mystery Tour

Words & Music by John Lennon & Paul McCartney

D A E G D/C G/B Gm/B
D/A B F♯m7 G♯m7 B7 A6 Dm7

Intro | D | A ||

E *Gesprochen:*
(Roll up, roll up for the Magical Mystery Tour,

Step right this way!)

Strophe 1

```
E             G                 A
  Roll up, ___ roll up for the Mystery Tour.
E             G                 A
  Roll up, ___ roll up for the Mystery Tour,
E
  Roll up, ___ (and that's an invitation,)
G                       A
  Roll up, ___ for the Mystery Tour.
E
  Roll up, ___ (to make a reservation,)
G                       A
  Roll up, ___ for the Mystery Tour.
```

Bridge 1

```
D                 D/C
  The Magical Mystery Tour
  G/B                      Gm/B♭
Is waiting to take you away,
D/A                    A
Waiting to take you away.
```

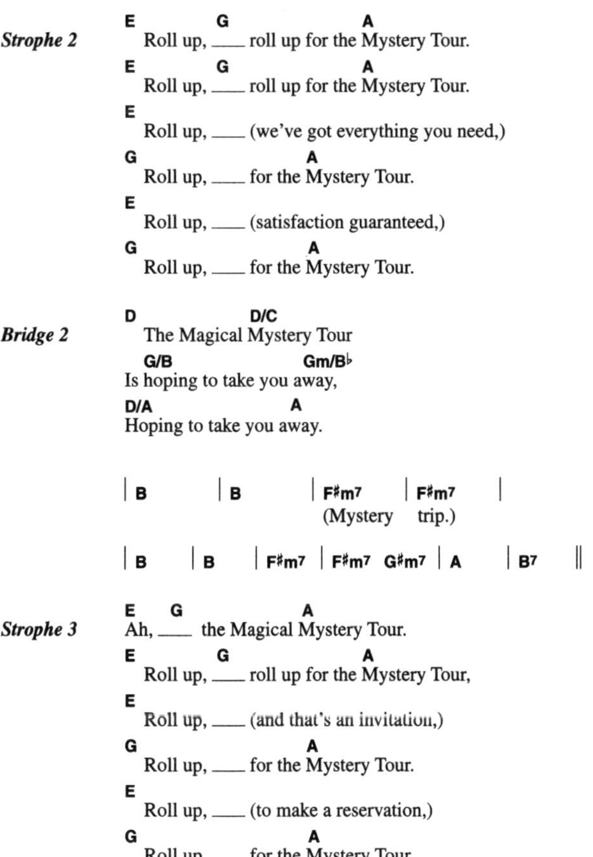

Strophe 2

E G A
Roll up, ___ roll up for the Mystery Tour.
E G A
Roll up, ___ roll up for the Mystery Tour.
E
Roll up, ___ (we've got everything you need,)
G A
Roll up, ___ for the Mystery Tour.
E
Roll up, ___ (satisfaction guaranteed,)
G A
Roll up, ___ for the Mystery Tour.

Bridge 2

D D/C
The Magical Mystery Tour
G/B Gm/B♭
Is hoping to take you away,
D/A A
Hoping to take you away.

| B | B | F♯m7 | F♯m7 |
(Mystery trip.)

| B | B | F♯m7 | F♯m7 G♯m7 | A | B7 ||

Strophe 3

E G A
Ah, ___ the Magical Mystery Tour.
E G A
Roll up, ___ roll up for the Mystery Tour,
E
Roll up, ___ (and that's an invitation,)
G A
Roll up, ___ for the Mystery Tour.
E
Roll up, ___ (to make a reservation,)
G A
Roll up, ___ for the Mystery Tour.

Bridge 3

```
D                 D/C
   The Magical Mystery Tour
   G/B                      Gm/B♭
Is coming to take you away,
D/A                        A6
Coming to take you away.
```

Bridge 4

```
D                 D/C
   The Magical Mystery Tour
   G/B                   Gm/B♭
Is dying to take you away,
D/A                     A6
Dying to take you away,
               D
Take you today. ____
```

Coda

```
| D       | D       ||

|: Dm7    | Dm7     | Dm7     | Dm7     :|
```

Repeat to fade

Michelle

Words & Music by John Lennon & Paul McCartney

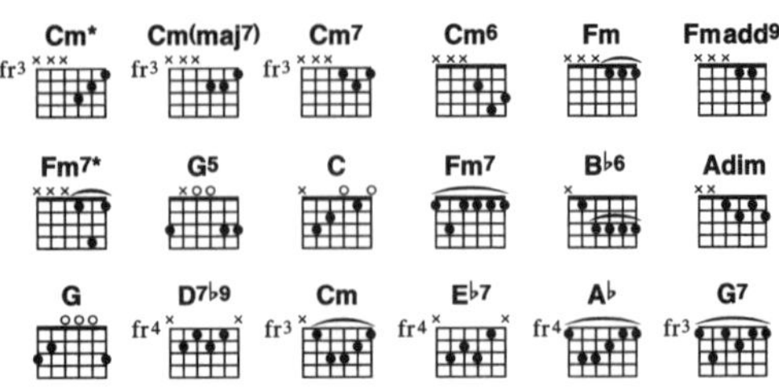

Kapo fünfter Bund

Intro | Cm* Cm(maj7) | Cm7 Cm6 | Fm Fmadd9 Fm Fm7* | G5 ||

Strophe 1

```
C           Fm7
Michelle,   ma belle,
B♭6                         Adim       G
These are words that go together well,
D7♭9    G
My Michelle.
```

Strophe 2

```
C           Fm7
Michelle,   ma belle,
B♭6                    Adim          G
Sont les mots qui vont très bien ensemble
D7♭9         G
Très bien ensemble.
```

Bridge 1

```
  Cm
I love you, I love you, I love you,
E♭7                  A♭
   That's all I want to say,
G7                 Cm
   Until I find a way,
        Cm*    Cm(maj7)  Cm7     Cm6
I will say the only       words I know
       Fm  Fmadd9  Fm  Fm7* G5
That you'll ___    un - der - stand.
```

Strophe 3 Wie Strophe 2

Bridge 2

```
Cm
I need to, I need to, I need to,
E♭7                        A♭
   I need to make you see,
G7                           Cm
   Oh, what you mean to me.
   Cm* Cm(maj7) Cm7   Cm6
Until I do I'm    hoping you
     Fm Fmadd9    Fm  Fm7* G5
Will know ______ what I     mean.
```

Solo

```
Cm             Fm7
   I love you. ____

| B♭6     | Adim     | G   D7♭9 | G       ||
```

Bridge 3

```
Cm
I want you, I want you, I want you,
E♭7                          A♭
   I think you know by now,
G7                         Cm
   I'll get to you somehow.
   Cm* Cm(maj7) Cm7   Cm6
Until I do  I'm   telling you,
   Fm Fmadd9      Fm Fm7* G5
So you'll ______  un - der - stand.
```

Strophe 4

```
C          Fm7
Michelle,  ma belle,
B♭6                 Adim          G
Sont les mots qui vont très bien ensemble
D7♭9       G
Très bien ensemble.
               Cm*     Cm(maj7)  Cm7     Cm6
And I will say the only          words I know
     Fm Fmadd9      Fm  Fm7* G5
That you'll ______  un - der - stand,
      C
My Michelle.
```

Solo

```
| Fm7     | B♭6     | Adim     | G   D7♭9 |

| Fm7     | B♭6     | Fade out
```

Norwegian Wood

Words & Music by John Lennon & Paul McCartney

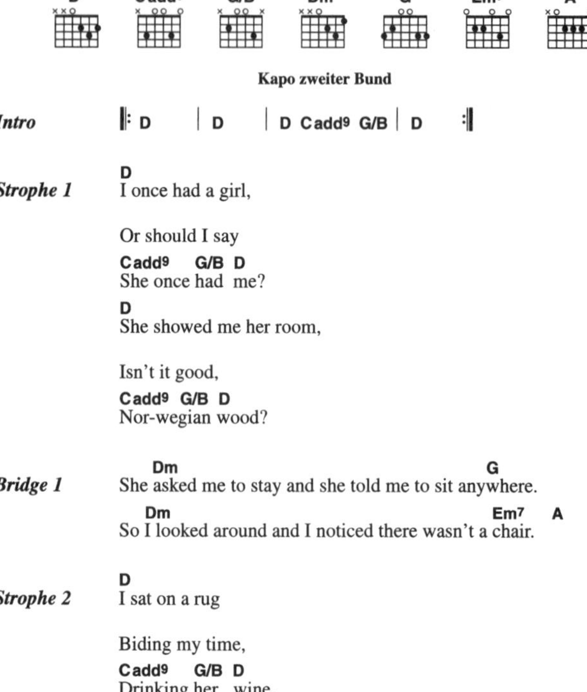

Kapo zweiter Bund

Intro |: D | D | D Cadd9 G/B | D :|

Strophe 1

D
I once had a girl,

Or should I say

Cadd9 G/B D
She once had me?

D
She showed me her room,

Isn't it good,

Cadd9 G/B D
Nor-wegian wood?

Bridge 1

Dm G
She asked me to stay and she told me to sit anywhere.

Dm Em7 A
So I looked around and I noticed there wasn't a chair.

Strophe 2

D
I sat on a rug

Biding my time,

Cadd9 G/B D
Drinking her wine.

cont.

```
D
We talked until two,

And then she said,
Cadd9    G/B D
„It's time for  bed."
```

Instrumental ‖: D | D | D Cadd9 G/B | D :‖

Bridge 2

```
    Dm                                                G
She told me she worked in the morning and started to laugh.
  Dm                                          Em7   A
I told her I didn't and crawled off to sleep in the bath.
```

Strophe 3

```
D
And when I awoke

I was alone,
Cadd9    G/B  D
This bird had  flown.
D
So I lit a fire,

Isn't it good,
Cadd9 G/B D
Nor-wegian wood?
```

Instrumental | D | D | D Cadd9 G/B | D ‖

Nowhere Man

Words & Music by John Lennon & Paul McCartney

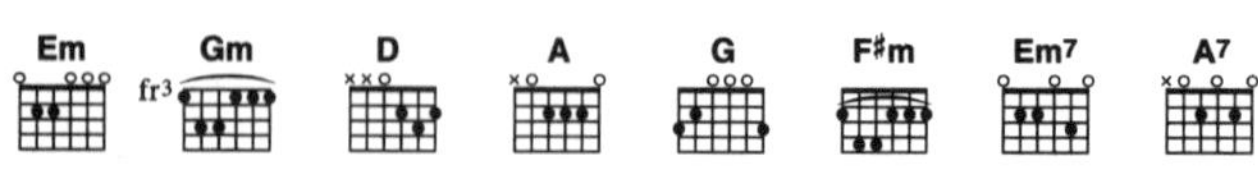

Kapo zweiter Bund

```
              N.C.
*Strophe 1*   He's a real Nowhere Man,

              Sitting in his Nowhere Land,
              Em             Gm               D
              Making all his Nowhere plans for nobody.

              D              A
*Strophe 2*   Doesn't have a point of view,
              G                     D
              Knows not where he's going to,
              Em         Gm           D
              Isn't he a bit like you and me?

                        F#m          G
*Bridge 1*    Nowhere Man, please listen,
                         F#m                G
              You don't know what you're missing,
                        F#m        Em7                      A7
              Nowhere Man, the world is at your command.

*Solo*        | D      | A      | G      | D      |

              | Em     | Gm     | D      | D      ||

              D               A
*Strophe 3*   He's as blind as he can be,
              G                    D
              Just sees what he wants to see,
              Em                    Gm             D
              Nowhere Man, can you see me at all?
```

```
             F#m        G
Bridge 2     Nowhere Man, don't worry,
                 F#m        G
             Take your time, don't hurry,
                 F#m  Em7                                A7
             Leave it all till somebody else lends you a hand.

             D              A
Strophe 4    Doesn't have a point of view,
             G                      D
             Knows not where he's going to,
             Em      Gm               D
             Isn't he a bit like you and me?

                     F#m        G
Bridge 3     Nowhere Man, please listen,
                     F#m                  G
             You don't know what you're missing,
                     F#m      Em7                        A7
             Nowhere Man, the world is at your command.

             D         A
Strophe 5    He's a real Nowhere Man,
             G           D
             Sitting in his Nowhere Land,
             Em             Gm                 D
             Making all his Nowhere plans for nobody.
             Fm             Gm                 D
             Making all his Nowhere plans for nobody.
             Em             Gm                 D
             Making all his Nowhere plans for nobody.
```

Ob-La-Di, Ob-La-Da

Words & Music by John Lennon & Paul McCartney

A E E7 D F#m7 A7 Asus2 A/E

Kapo erster Bund

Intro | A | A | A | A ||

Strophe 1

```
A                                     E
Desmond has a barrow in the market place,
E7                         A
Molly is a singer in a band.
                                    D
Desmond says to Molly, girl, I like your face,
          A                 E                 A
And Molly says this as she takes him by the hand.
```

Refrain 1

```
          A                   E   F#m7
Ob-La-Di, Ob-La-Da, life goes on, bra,
A           E       A
La-la how their life goes on.
          A                   E   F#m7
Ob-La-Di, Ob-La-Da, life goes on, bra,
A           E       A
La-la how their life goes on.
```

Strophe 2

```
A                                   E
Desmond takes a trolley to the jeweller's store,
E7                               A
Buys a twenty carat golden ring.
                                      D
Takes it back to Molly waiting at the door,
             A              E            A
And as he gives it to her, she begins to sing:
```

Refrain 2 Wie Refrain 1

Bridge 1

D
In a couple of years,

A $Asus^2$ A A^7
They have built a home sweet home.

D
With a couple of kids running in the yard

A/E E
Of Desmond and Molly Jones.

Strophe 3

A E
Happy ever after in the market place,

E^7 A
Desmond lets the children lend a hand.

D
Molly stays at home and does her pretty face,

A E A
And in the evening she still sings it with the band.

Refrain 3

Wie Refrain 1

Bridge 2

Wie Bridge 1

Strophe 4

A E
Happy ever after in the market place,

E^7 A
Molly lets the children lend a hand.

D
Desmond stays at home and does his pretty face,

A E A
And in the evening she's a singer with the band.

Refrain 4

A E $F\sharp m^7$
Ob-La-Di, Ob-La-Da, life goes on, bra,

A E A
La-la how their life goes on.

A E $F\sharp m^7$
Ob-La-Di, Ob-La-Da, life goes on, bra,

A E $F\sharp m^7$
La-la how their life goes on,

And if you want some fun,

E A
Take Ob-La-Di-Bla-Da.

Octopus's Garden

Words & Music by Ringo Starr

E A D B C♯m F♯m D♯

Intro B E B ‖ E C#m | A B ‖

Strophe 1

```
E                C#m
I'd like to be under the sea
         A                       B
In an octopus's garden in the shade.
E                C#m
He'd let us in, knows where we've been
         A                       B
In his octopus's garden in the shade.
```

Refrain 1

```
C#m
I'd ask my friends to come and see
A               B
An octopus's garden with me.
E               C#m
I'd like to be under the sea
         A             B          E
In an octopus's garden in the shade.
```

Strophe 2

```
E                        C#m
We would be warm below the storm
          A                          B
In our little hideaway beneath the waves.
E                   C#m
Resting our head on the sea bed
          A                      B
In an octopus's garden near a cave.
```

Refrain 2

C#m
We would sing and dance around
A B
because we know we can't be found.
E C#m
I'd like to be under the sea
A B E
In an octopus's garden in the shade.

Solo

| A | F#m | D | E |

| A | F#m | D E | A B ||

Strophe 3

E C#m
We would shout and swim about
A B
The coral that lies beneath the waves.
E C#m
Oh what joy for every girl and boy
A B
Knowing they're happy and they're safe.

Refrain 3

C#m
We would be so happy you and me,
A B
No one there to tell us what to do.
E C#m
I'd like to be under the sea
A B C#m
In an octopus's garden with you,
A B C#m
In an octopus's garden with you,
A B E D# E
In an octopus's garden with you.

Paperback Writer

Words & Music by John Lennon & Paul McCartney

G7 G C

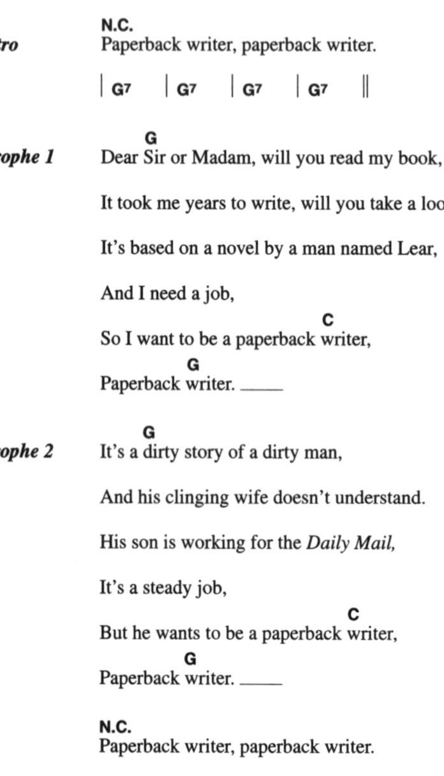

N.C.
Intro Paperback writer, paperback writer.

| G7 | G7 | G7 | G7 ||

Strophe 1
G
Dear Sir or Madam, will you read my book,
It took me years to write, will you take a look?
It's based on a novel by a man named Lear,
And I need a job,
C
So I want to be a paperback writer,
G
Paperback writer. ____

Strophe 2
G
It's a dirty story of a dirty man,
And his clinging wife doesn't understand.
His son is working for the *Daily Mail,*
It's a steady job,
C
But he wants to be a paperback writer,
G
Paperback writer. ____

N.C.
Paperback writer, paperback writer.

| G7 | G7 | G7 | G7 ||

Strophe 3

G
It's a thousand pages, give or take a few,

I'll be writing more in a week or two.

I can make it longer if you like the style,

I can change it round,

C
And I want to be a paperback writer,

G G7
Paperback writer. ____

Strophe 4

G
If you really like it, you can have the rights,

It could make a million for you overnight,

If you must return it, you can send it here,

But I need a break,

C
And I want to be a paperback writer,

G
Paperback writer. ____

N.C.
Paperback writer, paperback writer.

| G7 | G7 | G7 | G7 ||

Coda

G
|: Paperback writer, paperback writer. :| *Repeat to fade*

Penny Lane

Words & Music by John Lennon & Paul McCartney

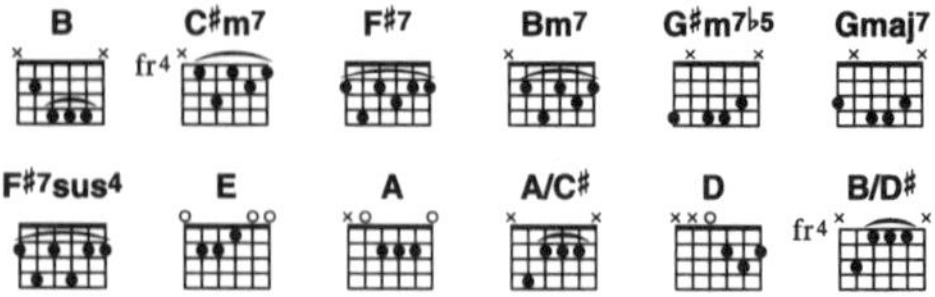

B C#m7 F#7 Bm7 G#m7♭5 Gmaj7

F#7sus4 E A A/C# D B/D#

Strophe 1

```
              B                                         C#m7      F#7
In Penny Lane there is a barber showing photographs
         B                                     Bm7
Of ev'ry head he's had the pleasure to know,
                G#m7♭5                 Gmaj7
And all the people that come and go,
                 F#7sus4  F#7  F#7sus4  F#7
Stop and say hello.
```

Strophe 2

```
            B                             C#m7     F#7
On the corner is a banker with a motorcar,
              B                                  Bm7
The little children laugh at him behind his back,
          G#m7♭5                    Gmaj7
And the banker never wears a mac
         F#7sus4       F#7    E
In the pouring rain,    –    very strange.
```

Refrain 1

```
        A              A/C#            D
Penny Lane is in my ears and in my eyes,
A                   A/C#          D
There beneath the blue suburban skies
          F#7
I sit, and meanwhile back…
```

Strophe 3

```
              B                                          C#m7      F#7
In Penny Lane there is a fireman with an hourglass,
               B                                   Bm7
And in his pocket is a portrait of the Queen.
```

cont.

G♯m7♭5 Gmaj7
He likes to keep his fire engine clean,
F♯7sus4 F♯7 F♯7sus4 F♯7
It's a clean machine.

Solo

| B | C♯m7 F♯7 | B | Bm7 |
| G♯m7♭5 | Gmaj7 | F♯7sus4 F♯7 | E ||

Refrain 2

A A/C♯ D
Penny Lane is in my ears and in my eyes,
A A/C♯ D
Full of fish and finger pies
F♯7
In summer, meanwhile back…

Strophe 4

B C♯m7 F♯7
Behind the shelter in the middle of the roundabout
B Bm7
The pretty nurse is selling poppies from a tray,
G♯m7♭5 Gmaj7
And though she feels as if she's in a play,
F♯7sus4 F♯7 F♯7sus4 F♯7
She is anyway.

Strophe 5

B C♯m7 F♯7
In Penny Lane the barber shaves another customer,
B Bm7
We see the banker sitting waiting for a trim,
G♯m7♭5 Gmaj7
And then the fireman rushes in
F♯7sus4 F♯7 E
From the pouring rain, – very strange.

Refrain 3

A A/C♯ D
Penny Lane is in my ears and in my eyes,
A A/C♯ D
There beneath the blue suburban skies
F♯7
I sit, and meanwhile back…
B B/D♯ E
Penny Lane is in my ears and in my eyes,
B B/D♯ E
There beneath the blue suburban skies…
B
Penny Lane.

Please Please Me

Words & Music by John Lennon & Paul McCartney

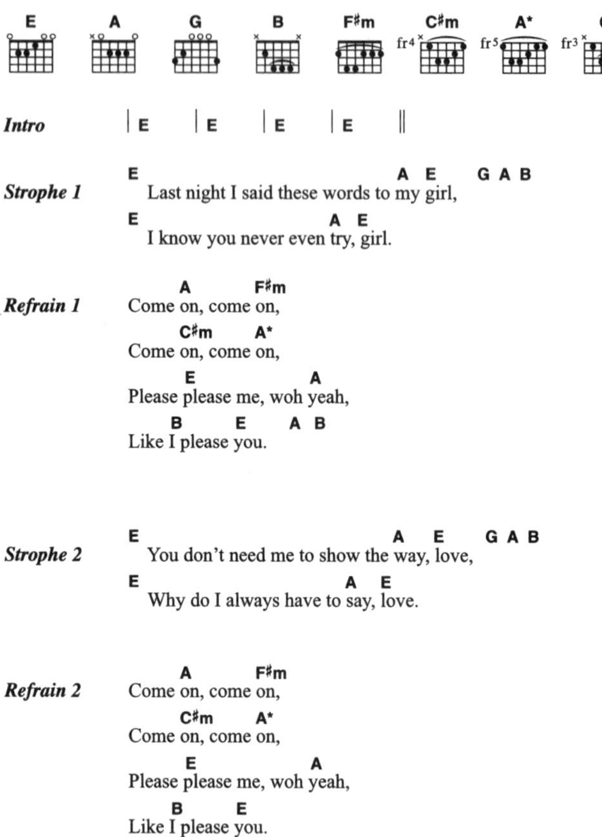

Intro | E | E | E | E ||

Strophe 1
E A E G A B
Last night I said these words to my girl,
E A E
I know you never even try, girl.

Refrain 1
A F#m
Come on, come on,
C#m A*
Come on, come on,
E A
Please please me, woh yeah,
B E A B
Like I please you.

Strophe 2
E A E G A B
You don't need me to show the way, love,
E A E
Why do I always have to say, love.

Refrain 2
A F#m
Come on, come on,
C#m A*
Come on, come on,
E A
Please please me, woh yeah,
B E
Like I please you.

Bridge

```
A
I don't want to sound complaining,
B                                   E
But you know there's always rain in my heart.
A
I do all the pleasing with you,
B                         E
It's so hard to reason with you,
   A        B               E      A  B
Oh yeah, why do you make me blue?
```

Strophe 3

```
E                                   A  E     G A B
  Last night I said these words to my girl,
E                          A  E
  I know you never even try, girl.
```

Refrain 3

```
     A        F#m
Come on, come on,
     C#m      A*
Come on, come on,
       E            A
Please please me, woh yeah,
      B
Like I please you.
E                   A
Please please me, woh yeah,
(you.)
      B
Like I please you,
E                   A
Please please me, woh yeah,
(you.)
      B      E    G  C  B  E
Like I please you. __________
```

Revolution

Words & Music by John Lennon & Paul McCartney

A E7 D E Bm G F#7

Intro | A | A | A | A | E7 ||

Strophe 1

```
     A
You say you want a revolution,
             D
Well, you know,
                          A
We all want to change the world.

You tell me that it's evolution,
             D
Well, you know,
                          E
We all want to change the world.
Bm                             E
   But when you talk about destruction,
Bm                              G    A  F#7    E
   Don't you know that you can count me out, in.
```

Refrain 1

```
                           A   D
Don't you know it's gonna be alright,
                           A   D
Don't you know it's gonna be alright.
                           A   D
Don't you know it's gonna be alright.
```

| E7 | E7 ||

Strophe 2

```
     A
You say you got a real solution,
             D
Well, you know,
                         A
We'd all love to see the plan.
```

cont. (Ba-oh shoo-be-doo-wop)

(Ba-oh shoo-be-doo-wop)

You ask me for a contribution,

```
               D
Well, you know,
                          E
We all do it when we can.
Bm                                        E
   But if you want money for people with minds that hate,
Bm                                  G    A  F#7  E
   All I can tell you is, brother, you have to  wait.
```

Refrain 2

```
                               A   D
Don't you know it's gonna be alright,
                               A   D
Don't you know it's gonna be alright.
                               A   D
Don't you know it's gonna be alright.

| E7    | E7    ||
```

Strophe 3

```
    A
You say you'll change the constitution,
               D
Well, you know,
                              A
We'd all love to change your head.
```

(Ba-oh shoo-be-doo-wop)

(Ba-oh shoo-be-doo-wop)

You tell me it's the institution,

```
               D
Well, you know,
                              E
You'd better free your mind instead.
```

(Ba-oh shoo-be-doo-wop)

(Ba-oh shoo-be-doo-wop)

```
Bm                                   E
   But if you go carrying pictures of Chairman Mao,
Bm                                        G    A   F#7   E
   You ain't gonna make it with anyone an - y - how.
```

```
                                               A    D
Refrain 3     Don't you know it's gonna be alright,
                                               A    D
              Don't you know it's gonna be alright.
                                               A    D
              Don't you know it's gonna be alright.

              | E7      | E7      ||

              A
Coda          (Oh shoo-be-doo-wop.)
              D
                Ah-ah-ah-ah,
              A         D
                Ah-ah-ah-ah,
                        A
              Ah-ah al - right,
                D       A
              Alright, alright,
                        D
              Alright, alright,
                        A
              Alright, alright!   ad lib. to fade
```

Rocky Raccoon

Words & Music by John Lennon & Paul McCartney

Am7 | D7sus4 | D7 | G7 | C | C/B

Intro | Am7 | Am7 ||

Strophe 1

```
      Am7
Now somewhere in the black mountain hills of Dakota
                D7sus4                       D7
There lived a young boy named Rocky Racoon-na
G7                                          C
And one day his woman ran off with another guy,
C/B                      Am7
Hit young Rocky in the eye,

Rocky didn't like that,
                D7sus4              D7
He said, „I'm gonna get that boy."
         G7
So one day he walked into town,
                                C           C/B
Booked himself a room in the local saloon.
```

Strophe 2

```
Am7                        D7sus4       D7
Rocky Racoon checked into his room,
G7                         C    C/B
Only to find Gideon's Bible.
Am7                  D7sus4            D7
Rocky had come, equipped with a gun,
   G7                             C      C/B
To shoot off the legs of his rival.
    Am7                      D7sus4        D7
His rival, it seems, had broken his dreams,
   G7                             C      C/B
By stealing the girl of his fancy.
    Am7                                  D7sus4          D7
Her name was Magill, and she called herself Lil,
    G7                            C      C/B
But everyone knew her as Nancy.
```

Strophe 3

Am7 D7sus4 D7
Now she and her man, who called himself Dan,
G7 C C/B
Were in the next room at the hoe-down.
Am7 D7sus4 D7
Rocky burst in, and grinning a grin,
G7 C C/B
He said, „Danny boy, this is a showdown."
Am7 D7sus4 D7
But Daniel was hot, he drew first and shot,
G7 C C/B
And Rocky collapsed in the corner.

Piano break

|: Am7 | D7sus4 D7 | G7 | C C/B :|

Strophe 4

Am7 D7sus4 D7
Now, the doctor came in, stinking of gin,
G7 C C/B
And proceeded to lie on the table.
Am7
He said, „Rocky, you met your match,"
D7sus4 D7
And Rocky said, "Doc, it's only a scratch,
G7
And I'll be better, I'll be better, Doc,
C C/B
As soon as I am able."

Strophe 5

Am7 D7sus4 D7
Now Rocky Racoon he fell back in his room,
G7 C C/B
Only to find Gideon's Bible.
Am7 D7sus4 D7
Gideon checked out and left in no doubt
G7 C C/B
To help with good Rocky's revival.

Piano break

| Am7 | D7sus4 D7 | G7 | C C/B |
(Do do do do do do do do do) etc.

Coda

| Am7 | D7sus4 D7 |
(Come on Rocky boy.) (Come on Rocky boy.)

| G7 | C G7 | C ||

Sexy Sadie

Words & Music by John Lennon & Paul McCartney

C D G F♯7 F D7

Bm Am7 Bm7 Cmaj7 A7 A♭7

fr3 fr5 fr4

Intro | C D | G F♯7 | F D7 ||

Strophe 1

G F♯7 Bm
Sexy Sadie, what have you done?
C D G F♯7
You made a fool of everyone, ____
C D G F♯7
You made a fool of everyone. ____
F D7 G
Sexy Sadie, oh, what have you done?

Strophe 2

G F♯7 Bm
Sexy Sadie, you broke the rules
C D G F♯7
You laid it down for all to see,
C D G F♯7
You laid it down for all to see. ____
F D7 G
Sexy Sadie, oh, you broke the rules.

Bridge 1

G Am7 Bm7 Cmaj7
One sunny day the world was waiting for a lover,
G Am7 Bm7 C
She came along to turn on everyone. ______
A7 A♭7 G
Sexy Sadie, the greatest of them all.

Strophe 3

G F♯7 Bm
Sexy Sadie, how did you know?
C D G F♯7
The world was waiting just for you, ____
C D G F♯7
The world was waiting just for you, ____
F D7 G
Sexy Sadie, oh, how did you know?

Strophe 4

G F♯7 Bm
Sexy Sadie, you'll get yours yet,
C D G F♯7
However big you think you are, ____
C D G F♯7
However big you think you are. ____
F D7 G
Sexy Sadie, oh you'll get yours yet.

Bridge 2

G Am7 Bm7 Cmaj7
We gave her everything we owned just to sit at her table.
G Am7 Bm7 C
Just a smile would lighten everything. ____
A7 A♭7 G F♯7
Sexy Sadie, she's the latest and the greatest of them all.

Coda

𝄆 Bm7 | C D | G F♯7 |
Ooh, ____

| C D | G F♯7 |
She made a fool of everyone, ____
How ever big you think you are, ____

| F D7 | G F♯7 𝄇 *Repeat to fade*
Sexy Sadie.
Sexy Sadie.

Sgt. Pepper's Lonely Hearts Club Band

Words & Music by John Lennon & Paul McCartney

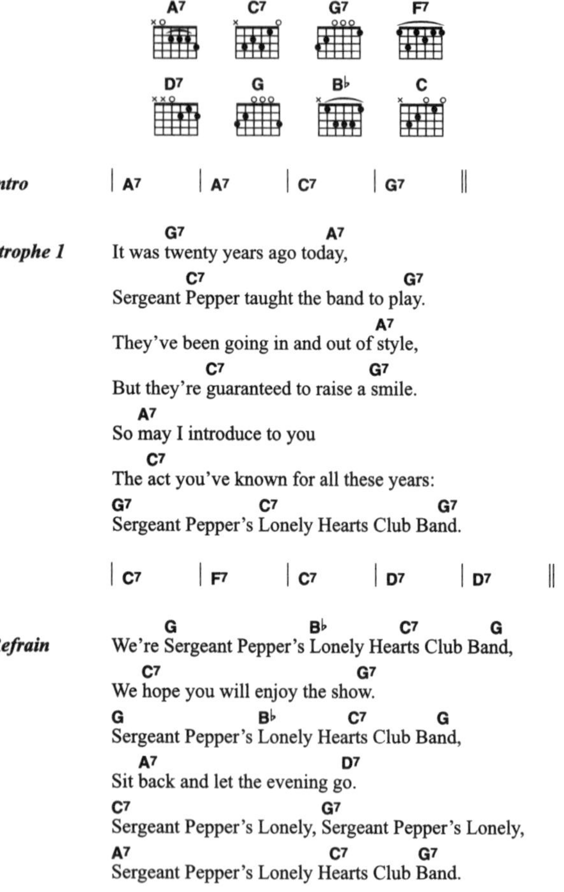

Intro | A7 | A7 | C7 | G7 ||

Strophe 1

G7 A7
It was twenty years ago today,
C7 G7
Sergeant Pepper taught the band to play.
A7
They've been going in and out of style,
C7 G7
But they're guaranteed to raise a smile.
A7
So may I introduce to you
C7
The act you've known for all these years:
G7 C7 G7
Sergeant Pepper's Lonely Hearts Club Band.

| C7 | F7 | C7 | D7 | D7 ||

Refrain

G B♭ C7 G
We're Sergeant Pepper's Lonely Hearts Club Band,
C7 G7
We hope you will enjoy the show.
G B♭ C7 G
Sergeant Pepper's Lonely Hearts Club Band,
A7 D7
Sit back and let the evening go.
C7 G7
Sergeant Pepper's Lonely, Sergeant Pepper's Lonely,
A7 C7 G7
Sergeant Pepper's Lonely Hearts Club Band.

Bridge

C7
It's wonderful to be here,
F7
It's certainly a thrill,
C7
You're such a lovely audience,
D7
We'd like to take you home with us,

We'd love to take you home.

Strophe 2

G7 A7
I don't really want to stop the show,
C7 G7
But I thought you might like to know,
A7
That the singer's going to sing a song,
C7 G7
And he wants you all to sing along.
A7
So let me introduce to you
C7
The one and only Billy Shears,
G7 C7 G7
And Sergeant Pepper's Lonely Hearts Club Band, yeah!

Coda

| C | C ||

She Loves You

Words & Music by John Lennon & Paul McCartney

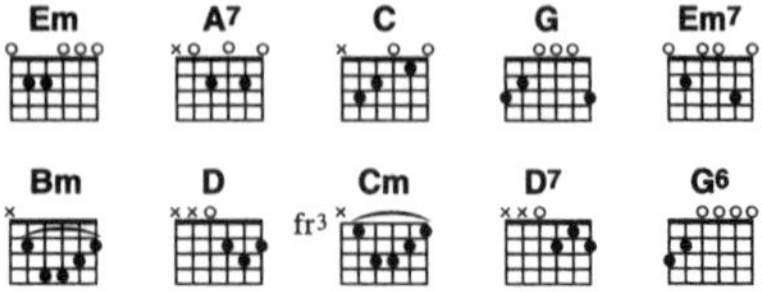

Em A7 C G Em7

Bm D Cm D7 G6

fr3

Intro

```
     Em
She loves you, yeah, yeah, yeah,
     A7
She loves you, yeah, yeah, yeah,
     C                          G
She loves you, yeah, yeah, yeah, yeah.
```

Strophe 1

```
     (G)              Em7
You think you lost your love,
       Bm            D
Well I saw her yesterday-yi-yay.
     G              Em7
It's you she's thinking of,
          Bm             D
And she told me what to say-yi-yay.
                G                                       Em
She says she loves you, and you know that can't be bad,
          Cm                                      D
Yes, she loves you, and you know you should be glad.
```

Strophe 2

```
     G              Em7
She said you hurt her so,
     Bm         D
She almost lost her mind.
     G                  Em7
But now she says she knows,
         Bm            D
You're not the hurting kind.
                G                                       Em
She says she loves you, and you know that can't be bad,
          Cm                                      D
Yes, she loves you, and you know you should be glad.   Ooh.
```

```
                   Em
*Refrain 1*        She loves you, yeah, yeah, yeah,
                   A7
                   She loves you, yeah, yeah, yeah.
                     Cm
                   With a love like that,
                   D7                 G
                   You know you should be glad.

                   G            Em7
*Strophe 3*        You know it's up to you,
                   Bm         D
                   I think it's only fair.
                   G               Em7
                   Pride can hurt you too,
                   Bm       D
                   Apologise to her.
                            G                                   Em
                   Because she loves you, and you know that can't be bad,
                          Cm                                  D
                   Yes, she loves you, and you know you should be glad.   Ooh.

                   Em
*Refrain 2*        She loves you, yeah, yeah, yeah,
                   A7
                   She loves you, yeah, yeah, yeah.
                     Cm
                   With a love like that,
                   D7                 G   Em
                   You know you should be glad.
                     Cm        N.C.
                   With a love like that,
                   D                  G   Em
                   You know you should be glad.
                     Cm        N.C.
                   With a love like that,
                   D7                 G
                   You know you should be glad.

                     Yeah, yeah, yeah,
                   C          G6
                   Yeah, yeah, yeah, yeah.
```

She's Leaving Home

Words & Music by John Lennon & Paul McCartney

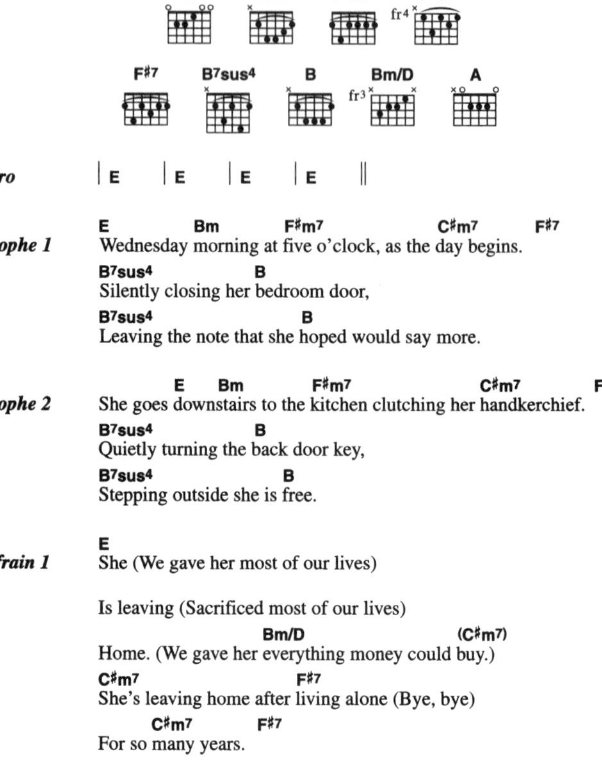

Intro | E | E | E | E ||

Strophe 1

E Bm F#m7 C#m7 F#7
Wednesday morning at five o'clock, as the day begins.
B7sus4 B
Silently closing her bedroom door,
B7sus4 B
Leaving the note that she hoped would say more.

Strophe 2

E Bm F#m7 C#m7 F#7
She goes downstairs to the kitchen clutching her handkerchief.
B7sus4 B
Quietly turning the back door key,
B7sus4 B
Stepping outside she is free.

Refrain 1

E
She (We gave her most of our lives)

Is leaving (Sacrificed most of our lives)
Bm/D (C#m7)
Home. (We gave her everything money could buy.)
C#m7 F#7
She's leaving home after living alone (Bye, bye)
C#m7 F#7
For so many years.

Strophe 3

E Bm F#m7 C#m7 F#7
Father snores as his wife gets into her dressing gown.
B7sus4 B
Picks up the letter that's lying there.
B7sus4 B
Standing alone at the top of the stairs.

Strophe 4

E Bm F#m7
She breaks down and cries to her husband,
C#m7 F#7
„Daddy, our baby's gone!"
B7sus4 B
„Why would she treat us so thoughtlessly?
B7sus4 B
How could she do this to me?"

Refrain 2

E
She (We never thought of ourselves)

Is leaving (Never a thought for ourselves)
Bm/D (C#m7)
Home. (We've struggled hard all our lives to get by.)
C#m7 F#7
She's leaving home after living alone (Bye, bye)
C#m7 F#7
For so many years.

Strophe 5

E Bm F#m7 C#m7 F#7
Friday morning at nine o'clock, she is far away.
B7sus4 B
Waiting to keep the appointment she made,
B7sus4 B
Meeting a man from the motor trade.

Refrain 3

E
She (What did we do that was wrong?)

Is having (We didn't know it was wrong)
Bm/D (C#m7)
Fun. (Fun is the one thing that money can't buy)
C#m7 F#7
Something inside that was always denied (Bye, bye)
C#m7 F#7
For so many years.
C#m7 F#7
She's leaving home.
A E
(Bye, bye.)

Strawberry Fields Forever

Words & Music by John Lennon & Paul McCartney

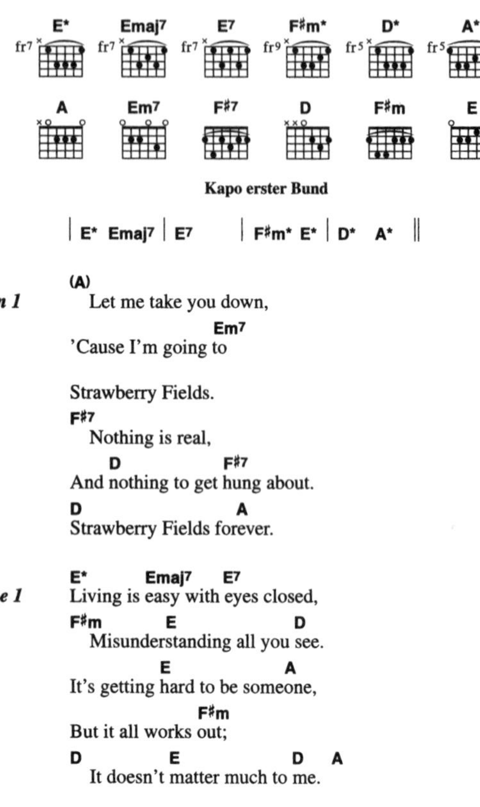

Kapo erster Bund

Intro | E* Emaj7 | E7 | F♯m* E* | D* A* ||

Refrain 1

```
(A)
   Let me take you down,
                        Em7
'Cause I'm going to

Strawberry Fields.
F♯7
   Nothing is real,
      D                  F♯7
And nothing to get hung about.
D                        A
Strawberry Fields forever.
```

Strophe 1

```
E*          Emaj7     E7
Living is easy with eyes closed,
F♯m           E                  D
   Misunderstanding all you see.
              E                  A
It's getting hard to be someone,
                      F♯m
But it all works out;
D              E                 D     A
   It doesn't matter much to me.
```

Refrain 2 Wie Refrain 1

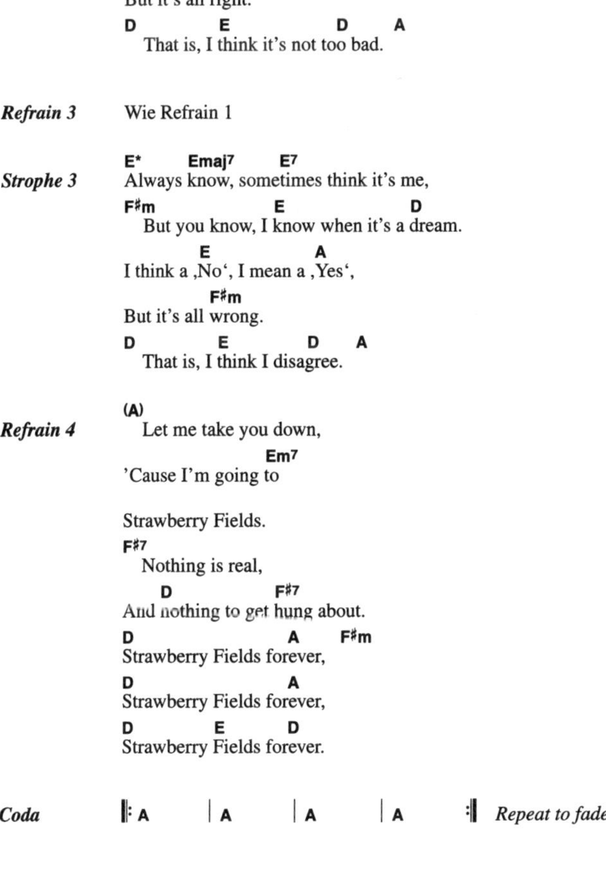

Strophe 2

E* Emaj7 E7
No-one I think is in my tree,
F♯m E D
I mean, it must be high or low.
E A
That is, you can't, you know, tune in,
F♯m
But it's all right.
D E D A
That is, I think it's not too bad.

Refrain 3

Wie Refrain 1

Strophe 3

E* Emaj7 E7
Always know, sometimes think it's me,
F♯m E D
But you know, I know when it's a dream.
E A
I think a ‚No', I mean a ‚Yes',
F♯m
But it's all wrong.
D E D A
That is, I think I disagree.

Refrain 4

(A)
Let me take you down,
Em7
'Cause I'm going to

Strawberry Fields.
F♯7
Nothing is real,
D F♯7
And nothing to get hung about.
D A F♯m
Strawberry Fields forever,
D A
Strawberry Fields forever,
D E D
Strawberry Fields forever.

Coda

‖: A | A | A | A :‖ *Repeat to fade*

Tell Me Why

Words & Music by John Lennon & Paul McCartney

Em7 A D Bm Em

A7 D7 G7 B♭7 Asus4 A6

Intro | Em7 A | Em7 A | Em7 A ||

Refrain 1

```
Em7 A      D
      Tell me why you cried,
Em7                   A       D  Em7
      And why you lied to me.
A        D
Tell me why you cried,
Em7                   A       D  Em7  A
      And why you lied to me.
```

Strophe 1

```
           D                        Bm
Well I gave you everything I had,
            Em                      A7
But you left me sitting on my own,
           D                        Bm
Did you have to treat me oh so bad?
         Em                      A7
All I do is hang my head and moan.
```

Refrain 2

```
A        D
Tell me why you cried,
Em7                   A       D  Em7
      And why you lied to me.
A        D
Tell me why you cried,
Em7                   A       D  Em7  A
      And why you lied to me.
```

```
                  D                            Bm
Strophe 2         If it's something that I've said or done,
                          Em                  A7
                  Tell me what and I'll apologise.
                       D                    Bm
                  If you don't, I really can't go on,
                           Em                    A7
                  Holding back these tears in my eyes.

                          D
Refrain 3         Tell me why you cried,
                  Em7                A      D  Em7
                       And why you lied to me.
                  A       D
                  Tell me why you cried,
                  Em7                A      D  D7
                       And why you lied to me.

                        G7
Bridge            Well I beg you on my bended knees,
                            A7
                  If you'll only listen to my pleas,
                          Bm
                  Is there anything I can do?
                             Em7
                  'Cause I really can't stand it,
                      A7             D
                  I'm so in love with you.

                  N.C.       D
Refrain 4              Tell me why you cried,
                  Em7                A      D  Em7
                       And why you lied to me.
                  A       D
                  Tell me why you cried,
                  Em7                A      Bm  B♭7  Asus4  A6  D
                       And why you lied to me.
```

Thank You Girl

Words & Music by John Lennon & Paul McCartney

A7 G D Bm Em

Intro | A7 | G ||

Strophe 1

A7 G
Oh, oh,
D G D G
You've ___ been good to me,
D A7 D G
You made me glad ___ when I was blue.
D G D G
And ___ eternally, ___
D A7 D
I'll always be ___ in love with you,

Refrain 1

G A7 G
And all I gotta do is thank you girl,
A7
Thank you girl.

Strophe 2

D G D G
I ___ could tell the world ___
D A7 D G
A thing or two ___ about our love.
D G D G
I ___ know little girl, ___
D A7 D
Only a fool ___ would doubt our love,

Refrain 2

G A7 G
And all I gotta do is thank you girl,
A7
Thank you girl.

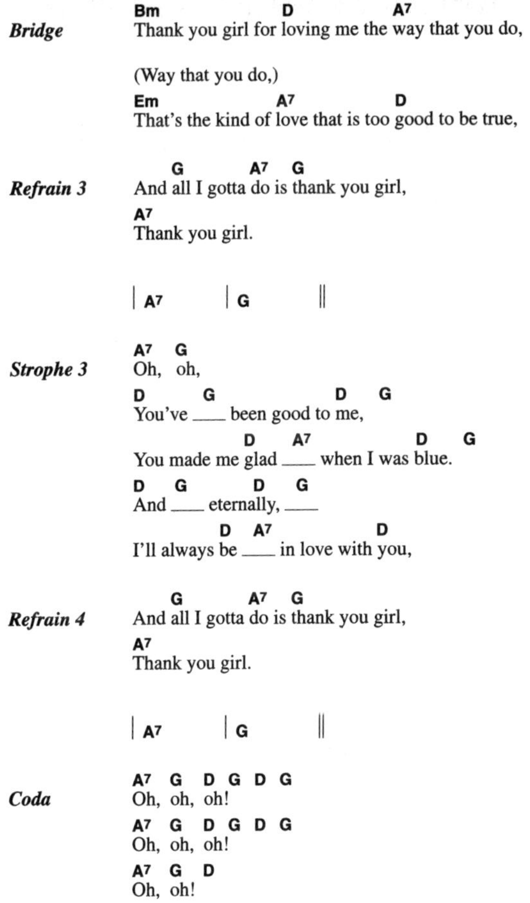

Bridge

```
Bm                 D              A7
Thank you girl for loving me the way that you do,

(Way that you do,)
Em                 A7             D
That's the kind of love that is too good to be true,
```

Refrain 3

```
    G         A7  G
And all I gotta do is thank you girl,
A7
Thank you girl.

| A7       | G        ||
```

Strophe 3

```
A7   G
Oh,  oh,
D      G              D    G
You've ___ been good to me,
              D    A7             D    G
You made me glad ___ when I was blue.
D   G        D   G
And ___ eternally, ___
           D  A7           D
I'll always be ___ in love with you,
```

Refrain 4

```
    G         A7  G
And all I gotta do is thank you girl,
A7
Thank you girl.

| A7       | G        ||
```

Coda

```
A7  G   D G D G
Oh, oh, oh!
A7  G   D G D G
Oh, oh, oh!
A7  G   D
Oh, oh!
```

The Ballad Of John And Yoko

Words & Music by John Lennon & Paul McCartney

E E7 A B7 E6

Intro | E | E ||

Strophe 1

```
E
Standing in the dock at Southampton,

Trying to get to Holland or France.
    E7
The man in the mac said,

„You've got to go back,"

You know they didn't give us a chance.
```

Refrain 1

```
                           A
Christ! You know it ain't easy,
                            E
You know how hard it can be.
                        B7
The way things are going,
                       E
They're gonna crucify me.
```

Strophe 2

```
E
Finally made the plane into Paris,

Honeymooning down by the Seine.
      E7
Peter Brown called to say,

„You can make it OK,

You can get married in Gibraltar, near Spain."
```

Refrain 2 Wie Refrain 1

Strophe 3

E
Drove from Paris to the Amsterdam Hilton,

Talking in our beds for a week.

E7
The newspeople said,

„Say what you doing in bed?“

I said, „We're only trying to get us some peace.“

Refrain 3 Wie Refrain 1

Bridge

A
Saving up your money for a rainy day,

Giving all your clothes to charity.

Last night the wife said,

„Oh boy when you're dead,

B7
You don't take nothing with you but your soul.“

Think!

Strophe 4

E
Made a lightning trip to Vienna,

Eating chocolate cake in a bag.

E7
The newspapers said,

„She's gone to his head,

They look just like two gurus in drag.“

Refrain 4

A
Christ! You know it ain't easy,

E
You know how hard it can be.

B7
The way things are going,

E
They're gonna crucify me.

Strophe 5

E
Caught the early plane back to London,

Fifty acorns tied in a sack.
E7
The men from the press said,

„We wish you success,

It's good to have the both of you back."

Refrain 5

A
Christ! You know it ain't easy,
E
You know how hard it can be.
B7
The way things are going,
E
They're gonna crucify me.

Coda

B7
The way things are going,
E
They're gonna crucify me.

| B7 | B7 | E | E6 ||

The Fool On The Hill

Words & Music by John Lennon & Paul McCartney

D6 Em/D Em7 A7

Bm7 Dm Dm aug C7 Dm7

Intro | D6 | D6 ||

Strophe 1

D6 Em/D
Day after day, alone on a hill,
D6 Em/D
The man with the foolish grin is keeping perfectly still.
Em7 A7
But nobody wants to know him,
D6 Bm7
They can see that he's just a fool.
Em7 A7
And he never gives an answer;

Refrain 1

Dm Dm aug Dm
But the fool on the hill
Dm aug
Sees the sun going down,
C7
And the eyes in his head
Dm Dm7 D6
See the world spinning round.

Strophe 2

D6 Em/D
Well on the way, his head in a cloud,
D6 Em/D
The man of a thousand voices talking perfectly loud.
Em7 A7
But nobody ever hears him,
D6 Bm7
Or the sound he appears to make.
Em7 A7
And he never seems to notice;

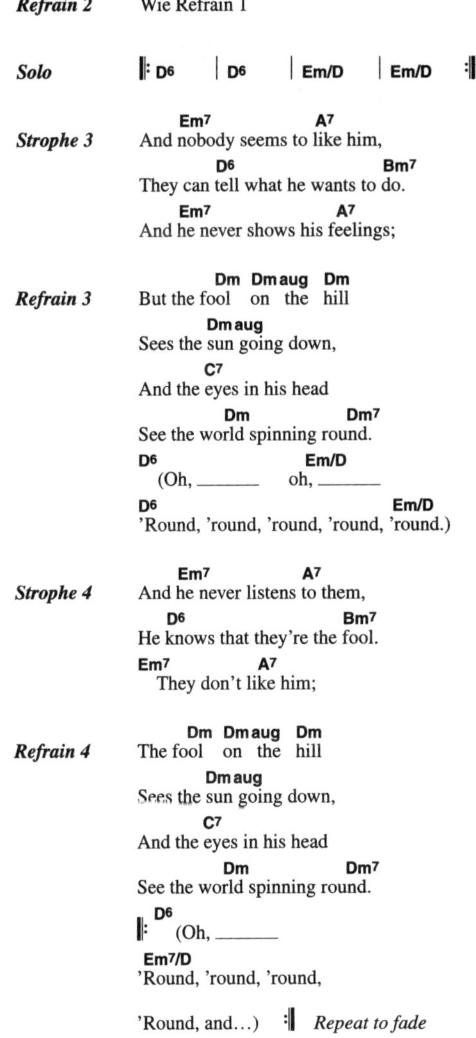

Refrain 2 Wie Refrain 1

Solo |: D6 | D6 | Em/D | Em/D :|

Strophe 3

Em7 A7
And nobody seems to like him,
D6 Bm7
They can tell what he wants to do.
Em7 A7
And he never shows his feelings;

Refrain 3

Dm Dmaug Dm
But the fool on the hill
Dmaug
Sees the sun going down,
C7
And the eyes in his head
Dm Dm7
See the world spinning round.
D6 Em/D
(Oh, ______ oh, ______
D6 Em/D
'Round, 'round, 'round, 'round, 'round.)

Strophe 4

Em7 A7
And he never listens to them,
D6 Bm7
He knows that they're the fool.
Em7 A7
They don't like him;

Refrain 4

Dm Dmaug Dm
The fool on the hill
Dmaug
Sees the sun going down,
C7
And the eyes in his head
Dm Dm7
See the world spinning round.
|: D6
(Oh, ______
Em7/D
'Round, 'round, 'round,

'Round, and…) :| *Repeat to fade*

The Long And Winding Road

Words & Music by John Lennon & Paul McCartney

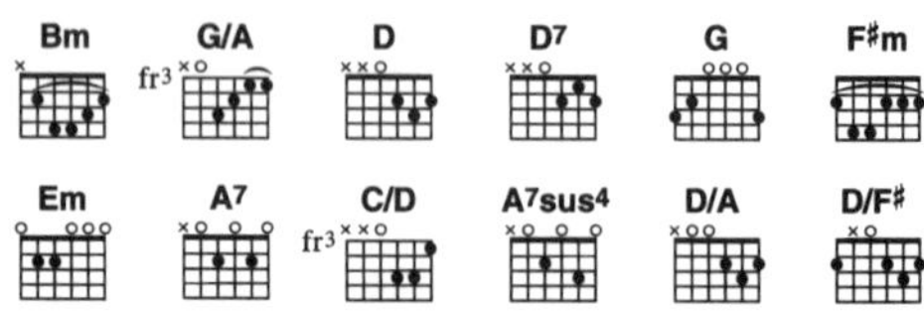

Kapo erster Bund

Strophe 1

```
     Bm                G/A
The long and winding road,
     D    D7       G
That leads to your door
     F♯m        Bm
Will never disappear.
Em                 A7       C/D
   I've seen that road before.
G    F♯m       Bm
   It always leads me here,
Em            A7  A7sus4  D
   Lead me to    your   door.
```

Strophe 2

```
     Bm                     G/A
The wild and windy night
              D   D7      G
That the rain washed away,
        F♯m  Bm
Has left a pool of tears
Em          A7       C/D
   Crying for the day.
G         F♯m          Bm
   Why leave me standing here?
Em      A7     A7sus4  D
Let me know the       way.
```

Bridge 1

D/A G
Many times I've been alone,
D/F# Em A7
And many times I've cried.
D/A G
Anyway, you'll never know
D/F# Em A7
The many ways I've tried.

Strophe 3

Bm G/A
And still they lead me back
D D7 G
To the long winding road.
F#m Bm
You left me standing here
Em A7 C/D
A long, long time ago.
G F#m Bm
Don't leave me waiting here,
Em A7 A7sus4 D
Lead me to your door.

Bridge 2

‖: D/A G | D/F# Em A7 :‖

Strophe 4

Bm G/A
But still they lead me back
D D7 G
To the long, winding road.
F#m Bm
You left me standing here
Em A7 C/D
A long, long time ago.
G F#m Bm
Don't keep me waiting here,
Em A7 D
Lead me to your door.
G/A D
(Yeah, yeah, yeah, yeah.)

The Word

Words & Music by John Lennon & Paul McCartney

D7#9 G7 Asus4 A

Gsus4 G D Cadd9 F

Intro | D7#9 | D7#9 ||

```
              D7#9
Refrain 1     Say the word and you'll be free,

              Say the word and be like me.
                  G7
              Say the word I'm thinking of,
                     D7#9
              Have you heard? The word is love.
                  Asus4  A        Gsus4  G
              It's so    fine, it's sun - shine,
                   D7#9
              It's the word love.


              D                       Cadd9
Strophe 1       In the beginning, I misunderstood,
              F                         G
                But now I've got it, the word is good.


                 D7#9
Refrain 2     Spread the word and you'll be free,

              Spread the word and be like me.
                     G7
              Spread the word I'm thinking of,
                     D7#9
              Have you heard? The word is love.
                  Asus4  A        Gsus4  G
              It's so    fine, it's sun - shine,
                   D7#9
              It's the word love.
```

Strophe 2

```
D                               Cadd9
   Everywhere I go I hear it said,
F                                                G
   In the good and the bad books that I have read.
```

Refrain 3 Wie Refrain 1

Strophe 3

```
D                                    Cadd9
   Now that I know what I feel must be right,
F                          G
   I'm here to show everybody the light.
```

Refrain 4

```
            D7#9
Give the word a chance to say,

That the word is just the way.
          G7
It's the word I'm thinking of,
            D7#9
And the only word is love.
     Asus4  A        Gsus4   G
It's so     fine, it's sun  -  shine,
          D7#9
It's the word love.
```

Solo

| D | Cadd9 | F | G | D7#9 | D7#9 ||

Coda

```
           D7#9
Say the word love,
           G7
Say the word love,
           D7#9
Say the word love,
           Asus4   A   Gsus4   G    D7#9
Say the word ______________________ love.
```

| D | Cadd9 | F | *Fade out*

There's A Place

Words & Music by John Lennon & Paul McCartney

Intro | E | A | E | A ||

Strophe 1

N.C.
There ______

E A E
Is a place where I can go,

A E
When I feel low,

C♯m B7
When I feel blue,

G♯m A*
And it's my mind, ______

E A
And there's no time ______

F♯m C♯m/G♯
When I'm alone.

Strophe 2

N.C.
I ______

E
Think of you

A E
And things you do

A E
Go round my head,

C♯m B7
The things you've said,

A B7
Like, I love only you. ____

Bridge

```
C#m                          F#
   In my mind there's no sorrow,
E                              G#7
   Don't you know that it's so?
C#m                        F#
   There'll be no sad tomorrow,
E                              G#7     C#m
   Don't you know that it's so?
```

Strophe 3

```
N.C.
There ______
     E    A               E
Is a place   where I can go,
A                 E
   When I feel low,
C#m               B7
   When I feel blue,
                 G#m     A*
And it's my mind, ______
                  E      A
And there's no time ______
         F#m  C#m/G#
When I'm alone.
```

Coda

```
N.C.        E       A
There's a place,
            E       A
There's a place,
            E       A
There's a place,
               E       A
|: There's a place.         :|   Repeat to fade
```

Things We Said Today

Words & Music by John Lennon & Paul McCartney

Am Em C C7 F

B♭ A D B7 E7

Intro | Am | Am ||

Strophe 1

```
Am          Em        Am           Em      Am
   You say you will love me if I have to go,
               Em       Am                  Em    Am
You'll be thinking of me, somehow I will know.
C                      C7
Someday when I'm lonely,
F                               B♭
Wishing you weren't so far away,
Am      Em     Am                      Em     Am
Then I will remember things we said today.
```

Strophe 2

```
Am       Em         Am                   Em     Am
You say you'll be mine, girl, till the end of time,
                  Em      Am                  Em     Am
These days, such a kind girl seems so hard to find.
C                         C7
Someday when we're dreaming
F                         B♭
   Deep in love, not a lot to say,
Am         Em      Am                      Em     A
Then we will remember things we said today.
```

```
            A                D
Bridge 1    Me, I'm just the lucky kind,
            B7                E7              A
            Love to hear you say that love is love,
                                D
            And though we may be blind,
            B7                Bb
            Love is here to stay.

            And that's:

              Am        Em        Am                 Em   Am
Strophe 3   Enough to make you mine, girl, be the only one.
                      Em     Am                  Em     Am
            Love me all the time, girl, we'll go on and on.
            C                    C7
            Someday when we're dreaming,
            F                  Bb
            Deep in love, not a lot to say,
            Am        Em     Am                     Em    A
            Then we will remember things we said today.


Bridge 2    Wie Bridge 1

              Am        Em        Am                 Em   Am
Strophe 4   Enough to make you mine, girl, be the only one.
                      Em     Am                  Em     Am
            Love me all the time, girl, we'll go on and on.
            C                    C7
            Someday when we're dreaming,
            F                  Bb
            Deep in love, not a lot to say,
            Am        Em     Am                    Em
            Then we will remember things we said to-day.

Coda        |: Am     | Am      | Am      | Am      :|  Repeat to fade
            (-day.)
```

This Boy

Words & Music by John Lennon & Paul McCartney

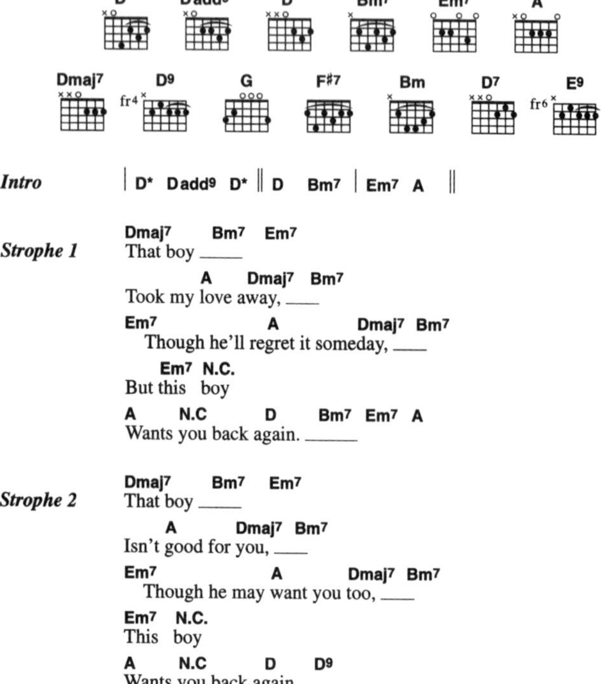

Intro | D* Dadd9 D* ‖ D Bm7 | Em7 A ‖

Strophe 1

Dmaj7 Bm7 Em7
That boy ____

A Dmaj7 Bm7
Took my love away, ____

Em7 A Dmaj7 Bm7
Though he'll regret it someday, ____

Em7 N.C.
But this boy

A N.C D Bm7 Em7 A
Wants you back again. ____

Strophe 2

Dmaj7 Bm7 Em7
That boy ____

A Dmaj7 Bm7
Isn't good for you, ____

Em7 A Dmaj7 Bm7
Though he may want you too, ____

Em7 N.C.
This boy

A N.C D D9
Wants you back again.

Bridge

```
         G                   F#7
Oh, and this boy would be happy,
        Bm                 D       D7
Just to love you, but oh my-hi-hi-hi-a,
G                    E9
That boy won't be happy
A                        N.C.
Till he's seen you cry. ___
```

Strophe 3

```
Dmaj7   Bm7  Em7
This boy ____
           A         Dmaj7 Bm7
Wouldn't mind the pain, ___
Em7                A      Dmaj7 Bm7
  Would always feel the same, ___
  Em7 N.C.
If this boy
A   N.C.       D     Bm7  Em7  A
Gets you back again.
```

Coda

```
Dmaj7 Bm7    Em7  A
This boy, __
   Dmaj7 Bm7    Em7  A
|: This boy, __            :|   Repeat to fade
```

Ticket To Ride

Words & Music by John Lennon & Paul McCartney

A Bm E F♯m D7 Gmaj7 E7

Intro | A | A | A | A ||

Strophe 1

```
A
I think I'm gonna be sad, I think it's today, yeah!
                                          Bm    E
The girl that's driving me mad is going away.
F♯m                 D7
She's got a ticket to ride,
F♯m                 Gmaj7
She's got a ticket to ride,
F♯m                 E                 A
She's got a ticket to ride, and she don't care.
```

Strophe 2

```
   A
She said that living with me was bringing her down, yeah!
                                        Bm     E
She would never be free when I was around.
F♯m                 D7
She's got a ticket to ride,
F♯m                 Gmaj7
She's got a ticket to ride,
F♯m                 E                 A
She's got a ticket to ride, and she don't care.
```

Bridge 1

```
 D7
I don't know why she's riding so high.

She ought to think twice,
                         E    E7
She ought to do right by me.
  D7
Before she gets to saying goodbye,

She ought to think twice,
                         E
She ought to do right by me.
```

Strophe 3

```
A
I think I'm gonna be sad, I think it's today, yeah!
                                             Bm    E
The girl that's driving me mad is going away, yeah!
    F♯m                D7
Ah, she's got a ticket to ride,
F♯m                Gmaj7
She's got a ticket to ride,
F♯m                E                   A
She's got a ticket to ride, and she don't care.
```

Bridge 2

```
 D7
I don't know why she's riding so high.

She ought to think twice,
                        E    E7
She ought to do right by me.
 D7
Before she gets to saying goodbye,

She ought to think twice,
                        E
She ought to do right by me.
```

Strophe 4

```
    A
She said that living with me was bringing her down, yeah!
                                           Bm    E
She would never be free when I was around.
F♯m                D7
She's got a ticket to ride,
F♯m                Gmaj7
She's got a ticket to ride,
F♯m                E                   A
She's got a ticket to ride, and she don't care.
   A
|: My baby don't care.   :|   Repeat to fade
```

Two Of Us

Words & Music by John Lennon & Paul McCartney

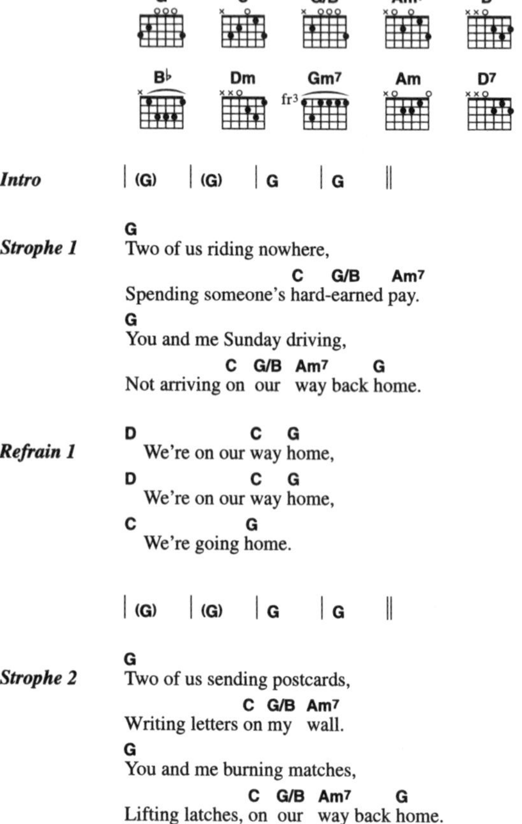

Intro

| (G) | (G) | G | G ||

Strophe 1

```
G
Two of us riding nowhere,
                          C    G/B    Am7
Spending someone's hard-earned pay.
G
You and me Sunday driving,
                 C   G/B  Am7       G
Not arriving on  our   way back home.
```

Refrain 1

```
D              C   G
   We're on our way home,
D              C   G
   We're on our way home,
C              G
   We're going home.
```

| (G) | (G) | G | G ||

Strophe 2

```
G
Two of us sending postcards,
                   C  G/B  Am7
Writing letters on my   wall.
G
You and me burning matches,
                    C   G/B  Am7       G
Lifting latches, on  our   way back home.
```

Refrain 2

D C G
We're on our way home,
D C G
We're on our way home,
C G
We're going home.

Bridge 1

B♭ Dm
You and I have memories,
Gm7 Am D7
Longer than the road that stretches out ahead.

Strophe 3

G
Two of us wearing raincoats,
C G/B Am7
Standing solo in the sun.
G
You and me chasing paper,
C G/B Am7 G
Getting nowhere on our way back home.

Refrain 3

D C G
We're on our way home,
D C G
We're on our way home,
C G
We're going home.

Bridge 2

B♭ Dm
You and I have memories,
Gm7 Am D7
Longer than the road that stretches out ahead.

Strophe 4

G
Two of us wearing raincoats,
C G/B Am7
Standing solo in the sun.
G
You and me chasing paper,
C G/B Am7 G
Getting nowhere on our way back home.

Refrain 4

Wie Refrain 3

Coda

| (G) | (G) |: G | G | G | G :| *Repeat to fade*

We Can Work It Out

Words & Music by John Lennon & Paul McCartney

D Dsus4 C G A

Bm Bm/A F#7sus4 F#7 Bm/G Bm/F#

Strophe 1

```
D                  Dsus4  D
  Try to see it my        way,
                  Dsus4              C            D
Do I have to keep on talking till I can't go on?
                     Dsus4  D
While you see it your       way,
                    Dsus4                C                    D
Run the risk of knowing that our love may soon be gone.
```

Refrain 1

```
G                  D
We can work it out,
G                  A
We can work it out. ___
```

Strophe 2

```
D                              Dsus4  D
  Think of what you're say   -   ing,
                     Dsus4                    C               D
You can get it wrong and still you think that it's alright.
                        Dsus4  D
Think of what I'm say   -   ing,
                         Dsus4            C                    D
We can work it out and get it straight, or say goodnight.
```

Refrain 2

```
G                  D
We can work it out,
G                  A
We can work it out. ___
```

Bridge 1

```
Bm                         Bm/A     G     F#7sus4
Life is very short, and there's no time ___
    F#7        Bm          Bm/A  Bm/G  Bm/F#
For fussing and fighting, my friend.
Bm                              Bm/A  G      F#7sus4
I have always thought that it's a   crime, ___
   F#7   Bm      Bm/A    Bm/G  Bm/F#
So I will ask you once a - gain.
```

Strophe 3

```
D               Dsus4  D
  Try to see it my     way,
                 Dsus4     C              D
Only time will tell if I am right or I am wrong.
                   Dsus4  D
While you see it your     way,
                         Dsus4         C                D
There's a chance that we might fall apart before too long.
```

Refrain 3

```
G                D
We can work it out,
G                A
We can work it out. ___
```

Bridge 2

Wie Bridge 1

Strophe 4

```
D               Dsus4  D
  Try to see it my     way,
                 Dsus4     C              D
Only time will tell if I am right or I am wrong.
                   Dsus4  D
While you see it your     way,
                         Dsus4         C                D
There's a chance that we might fall apart before too long.
```

Refrain 4

```
G                D
We can work it out,
G                A
We can work it out. ___

| D        | D        ||
```

When I'm Sixty Four

Words & Music by John Lennon & Paul McCartney

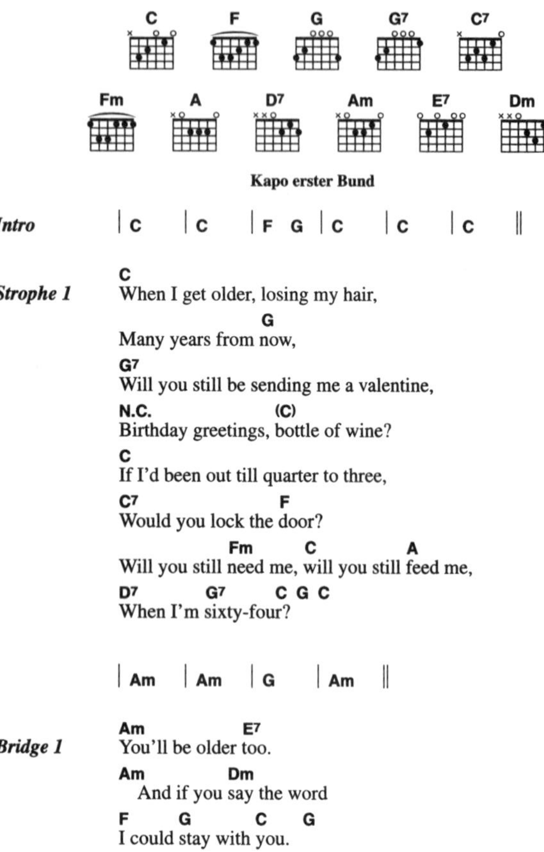

Kapo erster Bund

Intro | C | C | F G | C | C | C ||

Strophe 1

```
C
When I get older, losing my hair,
                   G
Many years from now,
G7
Will you still be sending me a valentine,
N.C.                  (C)
Birthday greetings, bottle of wine?
C
If I'd been out till quarter to three,
C7                    F
Would you lock the door?
              Fm        C              A
Will you still need me, will you still feed me,
D7          G7         C  G  C
When I'm sixty-four?
```

| Am | Am | G | Am ||

Bridge 1

```
Am                 E7
You'll be older too.
Am             Dm
   And if you say the word
F         G          C      G
I could stay with you.
```

Strophe 2

```
C
I could be handy, mending a fuse
                         G
When your lights have gone.
G7
You can knit a sweater by the fireside,
N.C.               (C)
Sunday mornings, go for a ride.
C
Doing the garden, digging the weeds,
C7                 F
Who could ask for more?
                 Fm        C               A
Will you still need me, will you still feed me
D7           G7        C G C
When I'm sixty-four?
```

Bridge 2

```
Am
Every summer we can rent a cottage
                G                        Am
In the Isle of Wight, if it's not too dear.
                          E7
We shall scrimp and save.
Am                Dm
   Grandchildren on your knee,
F     G          C       G
Vera, Chuck and Dave.
```

Strophe 3

```
C
Send me a postcard, drop me a line,
                    G
Stating point of view.
G7
Indicate precisely what you mean to say,
N.C.             (C)
Yours sincerely, wasting away.
C
Give me your answer, fill in a form,
C7          F
Mine for evermore.
                 Fm        C               A
Will you still need me, will you still feed me
D7           G7        C G C
When I'm sixty-four?
```

Coda

```
| C   | C   | F  G | C G C ||
```

With A Little Help From My Friends

Words & Music by John Lennon & Paul McCartney

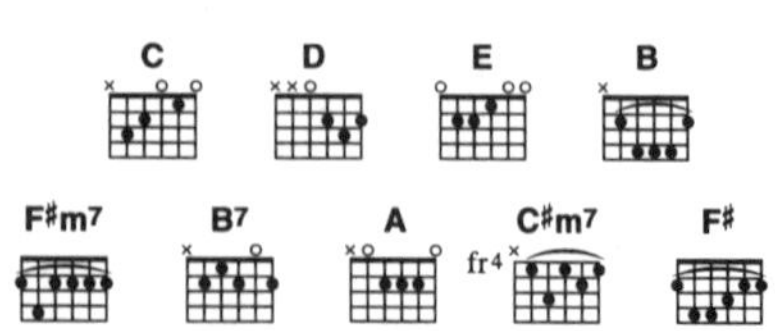


```
             C    D E
Intro        Bil - ly  Shears.

             E                   B             F♯m7
Strophe 1    What would you think if I sang out of tune,
                                         B7          E
             Would you stand up and walk out on me?
                              B              F♯m7
             Lend me your ears and I'll sing you a song,
                                 B7           E
             And I'll try not to sing out of key.

                       D                    A              E
Refrain 1    Oh, I get by with a little help from my friends,
                        D                    A              E
             Mm, I get high with a little help from my friends,
                                 A                                E         B
             Mm, I'm gonna try with a little help from my friends.

             E             B               F♯m7
Strophe 2    What do I do when my love is away?
                                        B7  E
             (Does it worry you to be alone?)
                           B            F♯m7
             How do I feel by the end of the day?
                                              B7          E
             (Are you sad because you're on your own?)
```

Refrain 2

D A E
No, I get by with a little help from my friends,
D A E
Mm, I get high with a little help from my friends,
A E
Mm, gonna try with a little help from my friends.

Bridge 1

C♯m7 F♯
Do you need anybody?
E D A
I need somebody to love.
C♯m7 F♯
Could it be anybody?
E D A
I want somebody to love.

Strophe 3

E B F♯m7
Would you believe in a love at first sight?
B7 E
Yes I'm certain that it happens all the time.
B F♯m7
What do you see when you turn out the light?
B7 E
I can't tell you, but I know it's mine.

Refrain 3

D A E
Oh, I get by with a little help from my friends,
D A E
Mm, get high with a little help from my friends,
A E
Oh, I'm gonna try with a little help from my friends.

Bridge 2

Wie Bridge 1

Refrain 4

D A E
Oh, I get by with a little help from my friends,
D A E
Mm, gonna try with a little help from my friends,
A E
Oh, I get high with a little help from my friends.
D A
Yes I get by with a little help from my friends,
C D E
With a little help from my friends. ___

Yellow Submarine

Words & Music by John Lennon & Paul McCartney

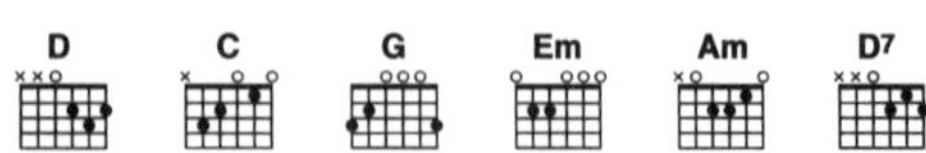

Tune guitar down one semitone

Strophe 1

D C G
In the town where I was born,
Em Am C D7
Lived a man who sailed to sea,
G D C G
And he told us of his life,
Em Am C D7
In the land of submarines.

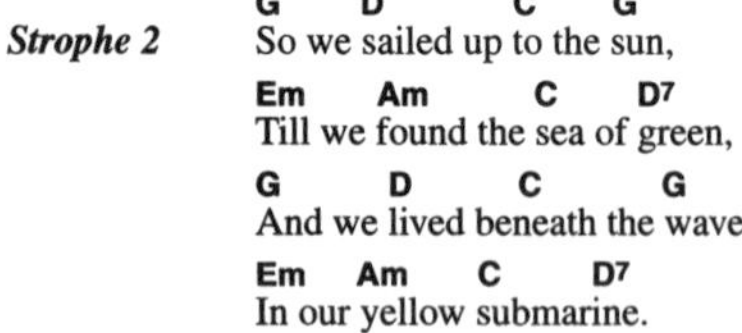

Strophe 2

G D C G
So we sailed up to the sun,
Em Am C D7
Till we found the sea of green,
G D C G
And we lived beneath the waves,
Em Am C D7
In our yellow submarine.

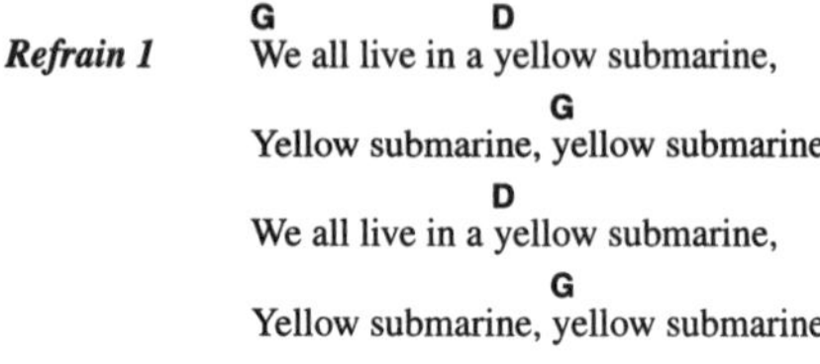

Refrain 1

G D
We all live in a yellow submarine,
G
Yellow submarine, yellow submarine.
D
We all live in a yellow submarine,
G
Yellow submarine, yellow submarine.

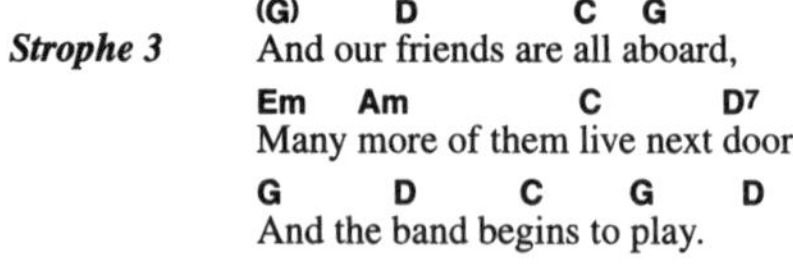

Strophe 3

(G) D C G
And our friends are all aboard,
Em Am C D7
Many more of them live next door,
G D C G D
And the band begins to play.

| G G | D7 G ||

Refrain 2

G D
We all live in a yellow submarine,
G
Yellow submarine, yellow submarine.
D
We all live in a yellow submarine,
G
Yellow submarine, yellow submarine.

Instrumental | D7 C | G Em | Am C | D7 G |

| D C | G Em | Am C | D7 G ||

Strophe 4

(G) D7 C G
As we live a life of ease,
Em Am C D7
Every one of us has all we need,
G D C G
Sky of blue and sea of green,
Em Am C D7
In our yellow submarine.

Refrain 3

G D
We all live in a yellow submarine,
G
Yellow submarine, yellow submarine.
D
||: We all live in a yellow submarine,
G
Yellow submarine, yellow submarine. :|| *Repeat to fade*

Yer Blues

Words & Music by John Lennon & Paul McCartney

E A7 G B7 A D E7

```
Strophe 1     E
              Yes, I'm lonely, wanna die,
              A7                E
              Yes, I'm lonely, wanna die,
              G
              If I ain't  dead already,
              B7                                    E    A  E  B7
              Whoo, girl, you know the reason why.

Strophe 2          E
              In the morning, wanna die,
                   A7              E
              In the evening, wanna die,
                       G
              If I ain't  dead already,
              B7                                    E    A  E  B7
              Whoo, girl, you know the reason why.

Bridge 1        E    N.C.
              My mother was of the sky,
              D      E  N.C.
                 My father was of the earth,
              D      E  N.C.
                 But I   am of the universe,
                    E7
              And you know what it's worth.

Strophe 3       A7             E
              I'm lonely, wanna die,
                       G
              If I ain't  dead already,
              B7                                    E    A  E  B7
              Whoo, girl, you know the reason why.
```

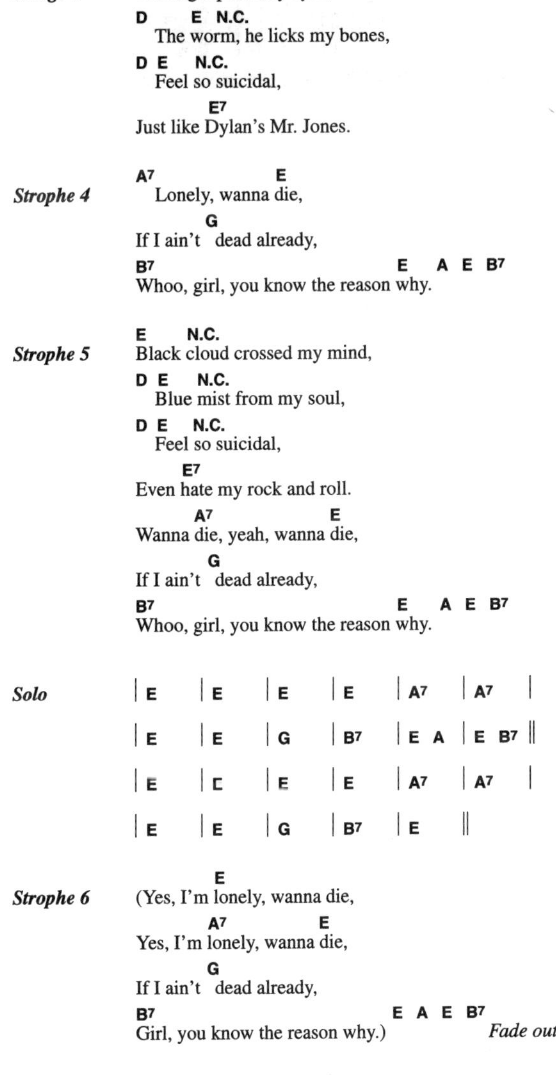

Bridge 2

E N.C.
The eagle picks my eyes,
D E N.C.
The worm, he licks my bones,
D E N.C.
Feel so suicidal,
E7
Just like Dylan's Mr. Jones.

Strophe 4

A7 E
Lonely, wanna die,
G
If I ain't dead already,
B7 E A E B7
Whoo, girl, you know the reason why.

Strophe 5

E N.C.
Black cloud crossed my mind,
D E N.C.
Blue mist from my soul,
D E N.C.
Feel so suicidal,
E7
Even hate my rock and roll.
A7 E
Wanna die, yeah, wanna die,
G
If I ain't dead already,
B7 E A E B7
Whoo, girl, you know the reason why.

Solo

E	E	E	E	A7	A7
E	E	G	B7	E A	E B7	
E	E	E	E	A7	A7
E	E	G	B7	E	

Strophe 6

E
(Yes, I'm lonely, wanna die,
A7 E
Yes, I'm lonely, wanna die,
G
If I ain't dead already,
B7 E A E B7
Girl, you know the reason why.) *Fade out*

Yes It Is

Words & Music by John Lennon & Paul McCartney

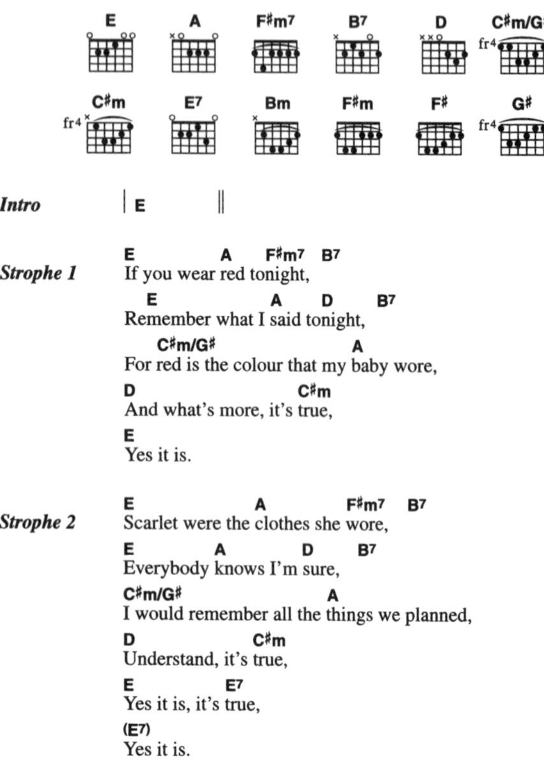

Intro | E ||

Strophe 1

E A F♯m7 B7
If you wear red tonight,
E A D B7
Remember what I said tonight,
C♯m/G♯ A
For red is the colour that my baby wore,
D C♯m
And what's more, it's true,
E
Yes it is.

Strophe 2

E A F♯m7 B7
Scarlet were the clothes she wore,
E A D B7
Everybody knows I'm sure,
C♯m/G♯ A
I would remember all the things we planned,
D C♯m
Understand, it's true,
E E7
Yes it is, it's true,
(E7)
Yes it is.

Bridge 1

```
Bm          E           A             F#m
I could be happy with you by my side,
Bm            E
If I could forget her,
    C#m
But it's my pride,
            E
Yes it is, yes it is,
             F#  B7
Oh yes it is,   yeah.
```

Strophe 3

```
E                      A       F#m7 B7
Please don't wear red tonight,
E               A      D       B7
This is what I said tonight,
    C#m/G#                          A
For red is the colour that will make me blue,
  D                    C#m
In spite of you, it's true,
E
Yes it is, it's true,
E7
Yes it is.
```

Bridge 2

Wie Bridge 1

Strophe 4

```
E                      A       F#m7 B7
Please don't wear red tonight,
E               A      D       B7
This is what I said tonight,
    C#m/G#                          A
For red is the colour that will make me blue,
  D                    C#m
In spite of you, it's true,
E             G#
Yes it is, it's true,
A             E
Yes it is, it's true.
```

Yesterday

Words & Music by John Lennon & Paul McCartney

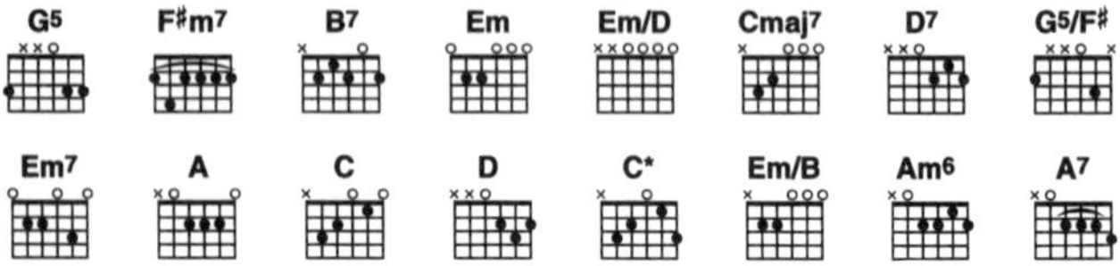

G5 F♯m7 B7 Em Em/D Cmaj7 D7 G5/F♯

Em7 A C D C* Em/B Am6 A7

Gitarre einen Ton tiefer stimmen

Intro | G5 | G5 ||

Strophe 1

G5 F♯m7
Yesterday,
B7 Em Em/D
All my troubles seemed so far away,
Cmaj7 D7 G5 G5/F♯
Now it looks as though they're here to stay,
Em7 A C G5
Oh, I be - lieve in yesterday.

Strophe 2

G5 F♯m7
Suddenly,
B7 Em Em/D
I'm not half the man I used to be,
Cmaj7 D7 G5 G5/F♯
There's a shadow hanging over me,
Em7 A C G5
Oh, yesterday came suddenly.

Bridge 1

F♯m7 B7 Em D C*
Why she had to go
Em/B Am6 D7 G5
I don't know, she wouldn't say.
F♯m7 B7 Em D C*
I said some-thing wrong
Em/B Am6 D7 G5
Now I long for yesterday.

Strophe 3

```
G5           F#m7
Yesterday,
           B7            Em            Em/D
Love was such an easy game to play,
Cmaj7   D7                 G5          G5/F#
  Now I need a place to hide away
     Em7  A        C  G5
Oh, I be - lieve in yesterday.
```

Bridge 2

```
F#m7  B7   Em   D  C*
Why   she  had  to go
Em/B    Am6        D7        G5
I   don't know, she wouldn't say.
F#m7  B7    Em    D    C*
I     said  some-thing wrong
Em/B  Am6       D7    G5
Now   I long for yesterday.
```

Strophe 4

```
G5           F#m7
Yesterday,
           B7            Em            Em/D
Love was such an easy game to play,
Cmaj7   D7                 G5          G5/F#
  Now I need a place to hide away,
     Em7  A        C  G5
Oh, I be - lieve in yesterday,
G  A7  C*  G5
Mmm. ______
```

You Can't Do That

Words & Music by John Lennon & Paul McCartney

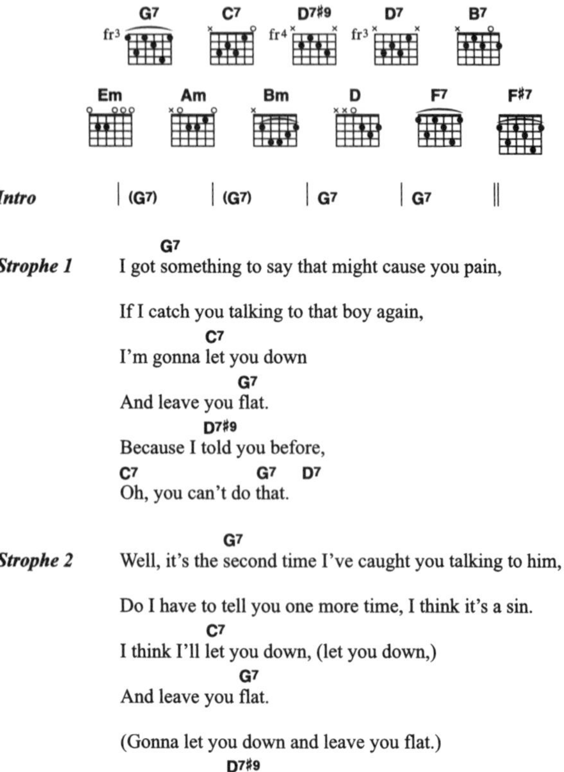

Intro | (G7) | (G7) | G7 | G7 ||

Strophe 1

G7
I got something to say that might cause you pain,

If I catch you talking to that boy again,
C7
I'm gonna let you down
G7
And leave you flat.
D7#9
Because I told you before,
C7 G7 D7
Oh, you can't do that.

Strophe 2

G7
Well, it's the second time I've caught you talking to him,

Do I have to tell you one more time, I think it's a sin.
C7
I think I'll let you down, (let you down,)
G7
And leave you flat.

(Gonna let you down and leave you flat.)
D7#9
Because I've told you before,
C7 G7
Oh, you can't do that.

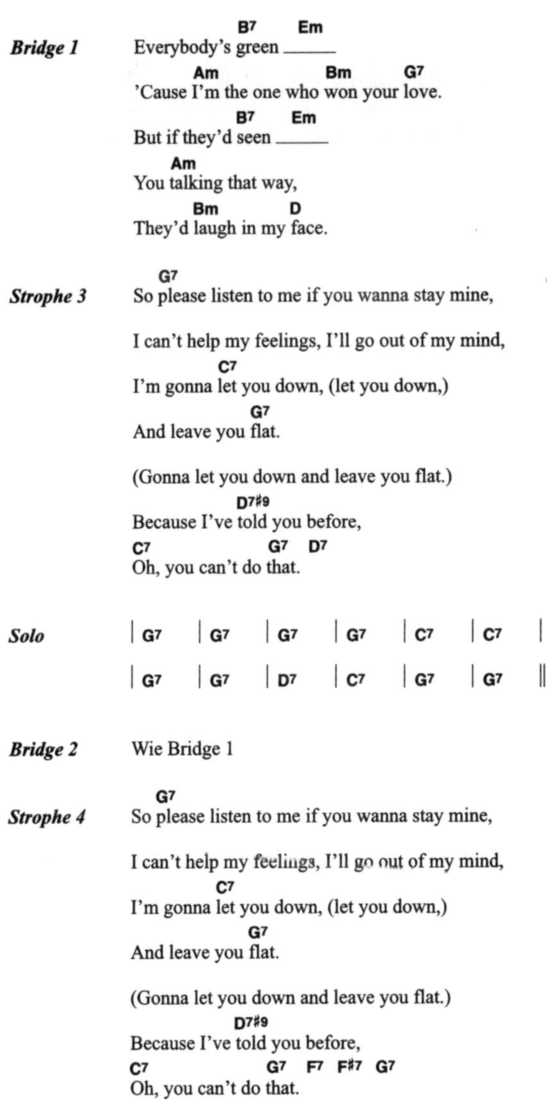

Bridge 1

```
                  B7      Em
Everybody's green ______
            Am                  Bm       G7
'Cause I'm the one who won your love.
                  B7     Em
But if they'd seen ______
        Am
You talking that way,
            Bm          D
They'd laugh in my face.
```

Strophe 3

```
   G7
So please listen to me if you wanna stay mine,

I can't help my feelings, I'll go out of my mind,
            C7
I'm gonna let you down, (let you down,)
                 G7
And leave you flat.

(Gonna let you down and leave you flat.)
                D7#9
Because I've told you before,
C7                 G7   D7
Oh, you can't do that.
```

Solo

G7	G7	G7	G7	C7	C7
G7	G7	D7	C7	G7	G7 ‖

Bridge 2

Wie Bridge 1

Strophe 4

```
   G7
So please listen to me if you wanna stay mine,

I can't help my feelings, I'll go out of my mind,
            C7
I'm gonna let you down, (let you down,)
                 G7
And leave you flat.

(Gonna let you down and leave you flat.)
                D7#9
Because I've told you before,
C7                 G7   F7   F#7   G7
Oh, you can't do that.
```

Your Mother Should Know

Words & Music by John Lennon & Paul McCartney

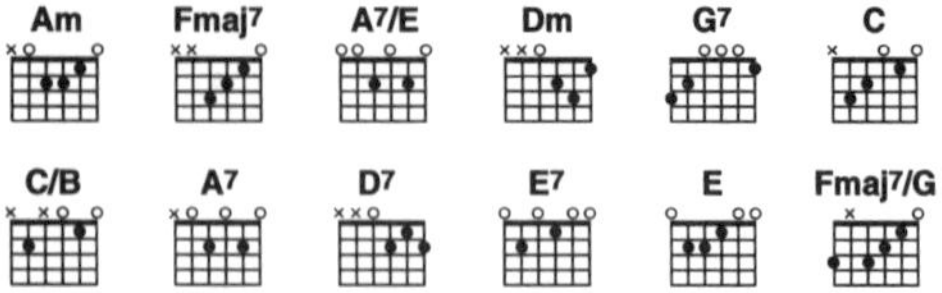

Am Fmaj7 A7/E Dm G7 C
C/B A7 D7 E7 E Fmaj7/G

Intro | Am | Am ||

Strophe 1

Am Fmaj7
Let's all get up and dance to a song
A7/E Dm
That was a hit before your mother was born.
G7 C C/B A7
Though she was born a long, long time ago,
D7
Your mother should know,
G7 C
Your mother should know.
E7
Sing it again.

Strophe 2

Am Fmaj7
Let's all get up and dance to a song
A7/E Dm
That was a hit before your mother was born.
G7 C C/B A7
Though she was born a long, long time ago,
D7
Your mother should know,
G7 C
Your mother should know.

| E | Am | Fmaj7 | Fmaj7 | Fmaj7/G | C | E7 ||

Strophe 3

```
Am                        Fmaj7
Lift up your hearts and sing me a song
             A7/E             Dm
That was a hit before your mother was born.
G7                          C          C/B    A7
Though she was born a long, long time ago,
                         D7
Your mother should know,
G7                          C
   Your mother should know.
A7                          D7
   Your mother should know,
G7                          C
   Your mother should know.
```

```
| E      | Am     | Fmaj7 | Fmaj7 | Fmaj7/G | C       |
E7
Sing it again…
```

Strophe 4

```
Am                 Fmaj7
Da da da da da, da da da da
           A7/E          Dm
Da da da, da da da da, da da da da.
G7                          C          C/B    A7
Though she was born a long, long time ago,
                         D7         G7
Your mother should know, (your mother should,)
                         C          A7
Your mother should know, ye - eah.
                         D7         G7
Your mother should know, (your mother should,)
                         C          A7
Your mother should know, ye - eah.
                         D7         G7
Your mother should know, (your mother should,)
                         C
Your mother should know, ye - eah.
```

You're Going To Lose That Girl

Words & Music by John Lennon & Paul McCartney

E C♯m F♯m B7 G♯ D G C F A

Refrain 1

(E)
You're gonna lose that girl,
(C♯m)
(Yes, yes, you're gonna lose that girl.)
(F♯m) (B7)
You're gonna lose ________ that girl,
(Yes, yes, you're gonna lose that girl.)

Strophe 1

E G♯
If you don't take her out tonight,
F♯m
She's gonna change her mind,
B7
(She's gonna change her mind.)
E G♯
And I will take her out tonight,
F♯m
And I will treat her kind.
B7
(I'm gonna treat her kind.)

Refrain 2

Wie Refrain 1

Strophe 2

E G♯
If you don't treat her right, my friend,
F♯m
You're gonna find her gone,
B7
(You're gonna find her gone,)
E G♯
'Cause I will treat her right and then
F♯m
You'll be the lonely one.
B7
(You're not the only one.)

Refrain 3

```
                      E
{ You're gonna lose that girl,                 C#m
{                         (Yes, yes, you're gonna lose that girl.)
                      F#m                    B7
{ You're gonna lose ________  that  girl,
{                     (Yes, yes, you're gonna lose that girl.)
                      F#m                                   D
  You're gonna lose ______ (yes, yes, you're gonna lose that girl.)
```

Bridge 1

```
G                  C                    G
   I'll make a point of taking her away from you,

(Watch what you do,) yeah.
                             C               F
The way you treat her, what else can I do?
```

Solo

```
|: E       | G#      | F#m      | B7      :|
```

Refrain 4 Wie Refrain 3

Bridge 2 Wie Bridge 1

Strophe 3 Wie Strophe 1

Refrain 5

```
                      E
{ You're gonna lose that girl,                 C#m
{                         (Yes, yes, you're gonna lose that girl.)
                      F#m                    B7
{ You're gonna lose ________  that  girl,
{                     (Yes, yes, you're gonna lose that girl.)
                      F#m        D     A   E
  You're gonna lose ________ that girl.
```

You've Got To Hide Your Love Away

Words & Music by John Lennon & Paul McCartney

G Dsus4 Fadd9 C

D D/C D/B D/A Dsus2

Strophe 1

```
G          Dsus4  Fadd9 C  G
  Here I stand,   head   in  hand,
C                      Fadd9   C
Turn my face to the wall.
G         Dsus4  Fadd9  C  G
If she's gone  I can't   go  on
C                  Fadd9  C   D
Feeling two foot small. _______
```

Strophe 2

```
G      Dsus4    Fadd9 C   G
Ev'rywhere   peo  -  ple stare,
C                  Fadd9 C
Each and ev'ry day.
G      Dsus4     Fadd9  C  G
I can see them laugh   at  me,
C                   Fadd9  C  D  D/C  D/B  D/A
And I hear them say: ___________
```

Refrain 1

```
G                     C                    Dsus4  D  Dsus2  D
Hey, you've got to hide your love away. ____
G                     C                    Dsus4  D  Dsus2  D
Hey, you've got to hide your love away. ____
```

Strophe 3

```
G          Dsus4 Fadd9 C  G
How can I        ev  - en try?
C            Fadd9  C
I can never win.
G          Dsus4 Fadd9 C  G
Hearing them, see - ing them
C              Fadd9  C  D
In the state I'm in. ____
```

Strophe 4

```
G             Dsus4 Fadd9 C  G
How could she       say   to me
C                Fadd9 C
Love will find a way?
G       Dsus4 Fadd9 C G
Gather round, all  you clowns,
C                 Fadd9 C D D/C D/B D/A
Let me hear you say: ______
```

Refrain 2

```
G                    C                 Dsus4 D Dsus2 D
Hey, you've got to hide your love away. ___
G                    C                 Dsus4 D Dsus2 D
Hey, you've got to hide your love away. ___
```

Solo

```
| G Dsus4 Fadd9  C  G | C    Fadd9 C |
| G Dsus4 Fadd9  C  G | C    Fadd9 C | G       ||
```